THE NEW
INDIAN SLOW COOKER

THE NEW
INDIAN SLOW COOKER

Recipes for Curries, Dals, Chutneys, Masalas, Biryani, and More

NEELA PANIZ

Photography by Eva Kolenko

TEN SPEED PRESS
Berkeley

TO MY *JAAN*!

Forty-four years and still going strong

ACKNOWLEDGMENTS **viii**

INTRODUCTION **1**

THE INDIAN KITCHEN **7**

23 BASICS AND ACCOMPANIMENTS

24 basmati rice

25 whole wheat flat breads

26 yogurt

27 chopped salad of tomatoes,
    cucumbers, and red onion

28 cucumber and yogurt raita

29 mint chutney

31 Indian fresh cheese

34 classic spice blend

37 SOUPS

38 chicken soup with rice, spinach,
    and tomatoes

40 sauteéd chicken with
    green mango powder

41 mulligatawny soup

42 tomato lentil soup

43 yogurt soup with daikon

45 CHUTNEYS

47 mixed dried fruit chutney

48 date and tamarind chutney

50 sweet tomato chutney

53 CURRIES

54 basic curry mix

55 boneless chicken curry

56 curried chicken frankies

57 braised chicken with dried fenugreek

59 cornish hens with rum and saffron

60 roast chicken à la rama

62 tomato-butter sauce

64 chicken kabobs in green spices

65 yogurt and black pepper chicken

67 kerala fish curry

69 fish with sautéed onion sauce

70 pork vindaloo

73 lamb chops with browned onions
    and tomatoes

75 browned lamb with onions,
    tomatoes, and spices

76 lamb with spinach

77 ground meat with potatoes and peas

79 VEGETABLES

80 cauliflower with ginger and cumin

83 kashmiri potato curry

84 green beans with mustard seeds and onion

85 eggplant with potatoes

86 eggplant with yogurt and saffron

88 sweet-and-sour eggplant

89 curried peas and indian cheese

90 spicy cabbage and peas

92 pureed spinach with indian cheese

94 potatoes and peas in tomato sauce

95 pumpkin with fennel and tamarind chutney

97 DALS

98 mercin's lemon dal

99 browned lentils with onions tomatoes, and ginger

100 yellow mung beans with fresh spinach

102 mixed yellow dal

103 green mung beans with browned onions

105 pink lentils with tomatoes and kari leaves

106 whole black lentils

107 chickpeas with vegetables

108 curried chickpeas

110 black-eyed pea curry

111 red kidney beans

113 RICE DISHES

115 basmati rice with browned onions

117 spiced rice with potatoes and peas

118 rice with chickpeas

119 mixed vegetable rice

120 chicken layered with rice

123 pink lentils and rice with mint

124 lamb layered with rice

126 green mung beans and rice

ABOUT THE AUTHOR 127

MEASUREMENT CONVERSION CHARTS 128

INDEX 129

acknowledgments

I would like to start by thanking Aaron Wehner of Ten Speed Press, whose phone call started this process. Over fourteen years ago, Ten Speed Press published *The Bombay Café* cookbook, and here they were offering me another book opportunity! But Indian food in a slow cooker: how was that going to work?

The journey has been enlightening and educational, and the support lent by my editor, Melissa Moore, has been invaluable; she has been there every step of the way. I spent the last few months of recipe testing and writing in India, and keeping in touch with Melissa via emails. Though we were oceans apart, it felt as if we were conversing across the table. Thank you.

To Lynn Alley, the author of *The Gourmet Vegetarian Slow Cooker* (part of a series of slow cooker books published by Ten Speed), for had I not read her book, I would still be pondering the decision to write this one. Thank you, Lynn; you have been a good friend, and a better teacher.

To Susan Pruett, whose recipe testing proved to be a great asset.

To my family in India, who watched me struggle at times with translating measures, ingredients, techniques, and other culinary matters from one culture to the other, for giving me the space I needed to write the book. I owe a big thank you to my younger sister, Radhika, an accomplished cook who opened her extremely well-staffed and well-stocked kitchen to me. She always found ways and means of meeting all my needs for testing the recipes. And thanks to her family, who readily sampled and critiqued the food that came out of this amazing machine.

To Gopi, Radhika's cook, *dhanyawad!* You interpreted the recipes through my instructions, and helped me prepare biryanis, soups, and a vegetable that I swore never to eat—pumpkin. I have to admit, Gopi, that the *kaddu ki sabzi* was delicious!

And, forever, to my parents, Kiki and Mohinder, who together with our cook Chandan set the highest standards of food while I was growing up. They taught me everything there is to know about combining flavors, textures, and even colors on the dining table. They were also my biggest fans, and I miss them tremendously!

To my children, Nikhil and Payal, along with their spouses, and my grandchildren, who still think that their grandmother is the world's best "cooker," a very big thank you. You have been my biggest supporters and critics, allowing me to test my recipes on you throughout the years.

And finally, this book would never have been finished if it were not for Franklin, my dear husband. The time you have so diligently spent working alongside me during the cooking, eating, and writing has proven to be invaluable. Your writing skills and experience as a producer and editor for television news helped define the final manuscript. You have been my most ardent fan as I have been yours. After forty-four years, you've kept with me with laughter, tears, and sanity. I am forever thankful for all those moments, *jaan;* let's keep writing together.

introduction

When I was asked if I would be interested in writing a book on Indian slow cooking, my immediate thought was that it was not possible to achieve in a slow cooker what one did in a saucepan. Indian food is based on slowly built combinations of spices and aromatics—you patiently brown the onions, fry the spices, roast the vegetables, tending to the pot to keep all moving along without sticking or burning. The slow cooker would be a new route to a crucial destination: the vibrant, deeply satisfying flavors of traditional curries, dals, chutneys, and more. I didn't know if it could be done.

My memories of Chandan, the cook my mother employed for over forty years, helped me decide to take the challenge. Chandan treated us to the most amazing meals full of vibrant flavors. He would buy fresh produce and meats from the market every day, seeking out the best quality and value. You could hear him, busy in the kitchen, butchering or grinding the meat, cleaning the poultry and seafood, and prepping the vegetables. And then there would be the sound of the spices being ground in a stone grinder. The bottom slab of stone had been pounded with small depressions to create a rough surface; the top, smaller stone resembled a thin brick. Chandan would sit on his haunches and grind dry spices between the stones, or make a paste of spices with ginger, garlic, and chiles. In the mid-1970s, on one of my visits home to India, I bought my mother a food processor, and Chandan could not have been more delighted to have this modern method of grinding his spices. Of course, it would never be quite the same as the stone grinder, but it saved his back. As time went on, more modern conveniences made their way into my mother's kitchen. When Chandan retired and Prem Singh took over the duties of the kitchen, I rarely saw the old *pathar* (stone) come out of its hiding hole. He was a modern cook, using the food processor, spice grinder, juicer, blender, and pressure cooker. I wager he would have made great use of a slow cooker.

I soon realized that since Indian food *is* slow cooking, the slow cooker makes sense. Dals are perfect in a slow cooker, especially those that need long cooking to break down into a creamy consistency. However, Indian recipes do require some additional steps to achieve the maximum flavor and stay true to the dish. We use many whole spices or seeds that need to be "popped" in hot oil or ghee. Meats, poultry, seafood, and some vegetables are stewed slowly in sauces, or masalas, which are in turn created by roasting spices combined with fresh aromatic ingredients such as ginger, garlic, onions, tomatoes, and coconut milk. For example, the base of many curries—the masala—starts with onions cooked to a deep, dark golden brown so that they may dissolve smoothly into the dish.

I was visiting with my family in India during the latter half of my research and recipe testing. I had one slow cooker shipped from the United States and, with much difficulty, located another in a store (as they said, "No one in India uses a slow cooker."). We borrowed a smaller one from a friend, for testing the chutneys; hers had sat on the top shelf of her kitchen, practically unused.

It was interesting to get the reactions of not only the family, who relished the dishes as they came out of the slow cookers, but also of the kitchen help, who found it fascinating that they could prep and then set the dish in the slow cooker on the counter and not have to worry about it again. There were times when we recognized that some of the textures differed, due to the lack of constant attention, but as a rule we were all awed by the flavors it produced—especially when the biryanis came out picture perfect. My sister's cook, Gopi, actually created the recipe for Pumpkin with Fennel and Tamarind Chutney on page 95; due to its deliciousness, and to his delight with the ease of its preparation, this dish was a winner.

Though there are many Indian cookbooks in the market, home cooks are often still wary of trying their hand at Indian food. Among other things, the standard Indian meal requires so many preparations to complete the plate: one must have either *chawal* (rice) or *chapattis* (flat breads), along with a curry (whether nonvegetarian or vegetarian), often a dal (stewed lentils or other legumes), and a raita (yogurt relish) or chutney as an accompaniment.

In this book, I have concentrated on offering you a variety of Indian regional curries, dals, chutneys, and vegetable side dishes that can work as sides for the curries; there are also some soups and rice dishes that can serve as the center of a meal. The assumption is that you are not going to have more than one slow cooker preparing varieties of dishes for a single meal, so a great many of these dishes can stand as the main dish in a meal, along with plain rice or *chapatti* (I have included recipes for these and other basics and accompaniments in the first chapter) and a relish or two. Note: I used a 6-quart slow cooker for testing almost all the recipes included in this book and have noted where the recipe can be halved and prepared in a smaller, 3½-quart slow cooker.

super slow cookers

While shopping for a new slow cooker
(my thirty-year-old one had disappeared—probably
sold off in a garage sale), I found to my delight that
technology has advanced. I discovered "super" slow
cookers: those that also allow stovetop cooking and oven
baking. Needless to say, I bought one. If you do invest in one of
these "multicook" slow cookers, you'll find that some of the steps
in these recipes can be done directly in the pot itself, stream-
lining the process. Don't worry, though, if your slow
cooker is more of a classic than state of the art: all the
recipes in this book can be made in a standard
slow cooker.

the Indian kitchen

The number of spices used in the Indian kitchen is huge. However, there are some that are a must—I've listed in this section the ones that are essential for making the recipes in this book. I recommend buying your spices from an Indian grocery store: because the merchandise turns over quickly, the spices are fresh; and because they are sold in bulk, you can buy as much as you need, which is economical. The best way to store spices is in airtight jars or containers—or in one or more *masala dabba* (see page 9).

In addition to spices, a well-stocked Indian pantry contains fresh vegetables, chiles, coconut milk, yogurt, nuts, rice, and various types of flour, lentils, and beans. Handy appliances for cooking Indian food in a modern kitchen include a food processor (to prep onions and other aromatics), a blender, a spice grinder and/or mortar and pestle, and heavy-duty nonreactive saucepans and stockpots—important since tomatoes, yogurt, and lemon juice are key ingredients in many recipes.

In the recipes in this book, some of the more unusual or specialized ingredients are marked with an asterisk (*), which means information about that item is found in this section.

masala dabba

Once you are at the Indian grocery store, invest in a
masala *dabba*—a round stainless steel container with seven
smaller containers with airtight lids and usually a small spoon.
I keep two at home: one smaller one for the whole spices and one
slightly larger one for the ground spices. (I would even recommend a third
if you store a lot of dried or ground non-Indian spices.) They are convenient as storage boxes and also allow you to take all the spices
to the stove, where you can spoon out as much as you need
into the cooking vessel without having to open and
close many bottles or jars.

SPICES, SPICE BLENDS, AND AROMATICS

ASAFETIDA (*hing*) is the dried resin of a perennial herb. Yellowish-brown and strong-smelling in its raw form, when cooked it lends an aroma and flavor of onion and garlic to many dishes. It's best if purchased in solid form and ground at home; the preground powder is cut with wheat and is weak in flavor. Store it in an airtight container to retain its potency and keep it from imparting its strong aroma to other spices.

In the West, **BAY LEAVES** come from the bay laurel tree; Indian bay leaves (*tej patta*), however, are from the cassia tree. Aromatic, pungent, and redolent of cinnamon, they are used in Roast Chicken à la Rama (page 60), Lamb Chops with Browned Onions and Tomatoes (page 73), and some of the other curries, too. Find them in Indian grocery stores or substitute regular bay laurel leaves.

BLACK PEPPER (*kali mirch*), native to Kerala in southwestern India, is widely available whole or ground—as with many spices, I advise that you buy the peppercorns whole and grind them at home.

BLACK SALT (*kala namak*) is used in Date and Tamarind Chutney (page 48) and Curried Chick-peas to bring a different level of saltiness, as it is highly sufuric in its compostion.

Whole **CARDAMOM PODS** (*illaichi*) are available green, which have a minty, herbaceous flavor, or black, which are more pungent.

CASSIA (*dalchini*), like its relative, true cinnamon, is the inner bark of a tree native to Asia. Both are sweet and aromatic; cassia is more pungent. In this book, they can be substituted for one another. For these recipes, you'll be using whole sticks rather than ground cassia.

CILANTRO (*hara dhania*) is the herb of choice for garnishing Indian dishes. To prepare it, wash the bunch of cilantro under cold running water. Gently shake off the excess water from the leaves and then place the bunch root side down in a drinking glass to allow the leaves to completely dry. Use the leaves and tender stems only for the garnish; the thicker stems close to the roots tend to be bitter. To store extra (washed and dry) cilantro, wrap it in a paper towel and then place it in a plastic bag.

CLOVES (*laung*) are the dried flower buds of an evergreen tree; aromatic and pungent, they are used whole or ground in spice mixes.

Grated **COCONUT** (*nariyal*) meat is available frozen in Indian and other Asian ethnic markets.

CORIANDER (*dhania*), the seeds of the same plant that yields the fresh herb cilantro (see above), is warm, citrusy, and sweet; buy the seeds whole and roast and grind them at home.

CUMIN (*zeera*) seeds, whether whole or ground, are used in dishes for their distinctive earthy, warming, slightly pungent flavor. As with other whole spieces, roasting them releases their oils and intensifies their flavor (see "Spice Preparation 101," page 12); roasted ground cumin keeps in an airtight jar for up to 10 days.

FENNEL SEEDS (*saunf*) bring a sweet anise flavor to dishes and spice blends.

FENUGREEK is a bitter herb, the seeds (*methi*) of which are used in Indian pickles; the dried leaves (*kasoori methi*) are used in many preparations to balance the flavors

GARAM MASALA is a classic blend of roasted and ground whole spices, which includes cardamom, cinnamon or cassia, cloves, coriander, cumin, black pepper, and whole red chiles. You can buy ready-blended garam masala, but it's best made at home (page 34).

Fresh **GINGER** (*adrak*), essential to many Asian cuisines, has found its place in Western markets. Several varieties of the rhizome are available: ethnic Asian and Indian markets sell the ginger imported from China or Indonesia, which tends to have less fiber than that available in supermarkets. When buying ginger, break off a piece to see how much fiber is there and choose a piece that has the least amount.

A small teaspoon is perfect for scraping the skin off gingerroot without peeling or paring off more than necessary. Most recipes will call for the rhizome to be measured by inches, which can be hard to judge, as some pieces are thinner than others. For the purposes of this book, a one-inch piece peeled and then minced is equivalent to a scant tablespoon. To julienne ginger, slice the peeled root at a bias creating long oval slices, then turn them 90 degrees and slice them into long thin strips. Ginger powder (*saunth*) is sharp, spicy, and aromatic.

spice preparation 101

Some recipes will call for roasting whole spices and then grinding them. The simplest and most efficient way to do this is to use a dry skillet. Place the whole spices in the skillet and roast them over medium-high heat, shaking continuously to get an even browning. As the spices roast, they will send forth an intense aroma and, depending on the spices you are roasting, they will deepen in color—especially cumin and coriander seeds. Whole red chiles will tend to burn if you're not careful; constant shaking of the skillet helps them roast evenly. As soon as they're roasted, transfer the spices from the hot skillet to a flat plate, spread them out to cool, and set aside.

To grind spices, use either a mortar and pestle (for a small amount) or a spice grinder—usually a coffee grinder that is dedicated to grinding spices (never coffee). Always store unused ground spices in an airtight jar or container (see page 9) and use them as soon as you can.

Many recipes in Indian cooking call for adding whole spices, such as cassia sticks, whole cloves, and bay leaves to the dish while it's cooking. These are for flavor but not consumption: remove them before serving the dish.

GREEN MANGO POWDER (*amchur*), tart and fruity, is available in Indian grocery stores and is used to add acid profile to a recipe in place of lemon or lime juice. However, lemon or lime juice cannot be substituted, as more often than not the acidity is required in a nonliquid form.

INDIAN RED CHILE is available whole (*sabut lal mirch*) or ground (*lal mirch*)—it's either hot or very hot, and deep red in color. (Pictured on page 4.) For whole, you can substitute árbol chiles; for ground, you can substitute cayenne. (Serrano chiles are closest to the flavor and pungency of the green chiles used in India.) I do not seed my chiles; if you prefer your food less spicy, remove the seeds. If you prefer your food really spicy leave the seeds in, or substitute Thai bird's eye chiles. It is best to use gloves when handling chiles.

JAGGERY (*gur*) is unrefined sugar (usually date, cane, or palm sugar) with a caramel flavor; it's sold in blocks in Indian grocery stores. You may substitute golden brown sugar, if you can't find jaggery.

KARI LEAVES (*meethi neem*), the aromatic leaves of the sweet neem tree, are available fresh in Indian markets. They add a fresh verdant flavor to the dish, and although they are best used fresh, neem leaves can be bought dried. Unlike bay leaves, they can be left in the food.

MACE (*jawantri*) is the covering of the nutmeg seed (see below), separated after harvest and sold as a spice on its own; its uses and flavors are similar.

MADRAS CURRY POWDER, a blend of roasted spices, such as coriander, mustard, and fenugreek, is used frequently in the curries of Southern India.

MUSTARD SEEDS (*rai*), tiny and round, are sharp and full of a strong flavor that mellows and becomes more complex when the seeds are roasted. I prefer the brown Indian variety, but you can substitute black Indian mustard seeds.

NIGELLA seeds (*kalonji*), sometimes sold as onion seeds (no relationship) are tiny black seeds with a flavor reminiscent of onion, oregano, and pepper.

NUTMEG (*jaiphal*), the spice, is the dried seed of the nutmeg tree. Warm, with a balance of sweet and bitter, it's used in small quantities. Though typically available ground, it's best when freshly grated, so buy a whole nutmeg (they're about the size of an olive) and grate off a bit when you need some.

PANCH PURAN is a five-spice mix made entirely of whole seeds: cumin, fennel, fenugreek, mustard, and nigella.

PANDANUS ESSENCE (*kewra*), distilled from the flower of the pandanus tree, is a sweet and aromatic addition to drinks and desserts—it's used like rosewater or orange-flower water.

Dried **POMEGRANATE SEEDS** (*anardana*) are tart and fruity, and are available whole or ground. I prefer to buy them ground, as they are difficult to grind and hard to chew when whole.

RASAM POWDER is a packaged spice mix for South Indian tomato soup, containing roasted *channa dal*, coriander, mustard, red chile, asafetida, and kari leaves. It's available in Indian markets.

SAFFRON (*kesar*), floral and aromatic, is the dried stigmas of the saffron crocus flower. This spice is very expensive, and is used sparingly to season and color dishes.

STAR ANISE (*chakri phool*), the sweet and fragrant dried fruit of an evergreen tree, smells and tastes like anise or fennel, though the plants are unrelated. Buy it whole, in pieces, or ground.

TAMARIND (*imli*) is available as pulp, which comes in blocks, and paste, which comes in jars, in Indian, Southeast Asian, Caribbean, and some Latino markets and specialty stores. To extract paste from pulp, break the pulp into pieces and soak it in boiling water. When the water is cool enough to handle, mash the pulp with your fingers and force it through a fine-mesh sieve to yield the paste.

TURMERIC (*haldi*) is a rhizome from the ginger family. Dried and ground, turmeric adds a warm and bitter flavor to a recipe. It has many health benefits and is considered a natural food preservative.

OTHER INGREDIENTS

BASMATI RICE is the choice when it comes to Indian cooking. Though many stores today carry basmati rice, it is not always imported from India or Pakistan—make the effort to find an imported basmati rice: there's a huge difference. Also, purchase basmati rice that is marked "aged" as it has less starch, resulting in a fluffier rice dish.

CHICKPEA FLOUR (*besan*), ground from chickpeas (*channa dal*), is used in breads and to thicken curries and many other dishes. It has an addictive earthy, nutty flavor; buy it in Indian markets and gourmet and specialty stores.

GHEE, or Indian clarified butter, is one of the primary cooking fats for Indian dishes. Made by cooking butter and removing the residue so that the end product is pure fat, ghee is shelf-stable and can be stored without refrigeration as long as it's in an airtight container. It's readily available in Indian and specialty markets.

SOFT WHOLE WHEAT PASTRY FLOUR (*atta*), is available in Indian grocery stores. If you cannot find *atta*, substitute soft whole wheat pastry flour. The chapatti will be a little denser due to the fact that *atta* is cut with a little bit of all-purpose flour.

LENTILS AND BEANS

Always pick through all legumes and beans for stones and twigs. Then rinse in several changes of cold water until the water runs almost clear. The beauty of the slow cooker is that you usually do not need to soak lentils or beans before cooking them.

There are many varieties of lentils and beans used in Indian cuisine. Here is a short description of those used in this book:

BLACK-EYED PEAS (*lobia*), are widely grown in Asia and provide a great source of protein, making them perfect in main courses for vegetarians.

BLACK LENTILS (*ma sabat*) are creamy and rich, and a favorite of Punjabis. These hearty lentils are best suited for the slow cooker as they require a lengthy stewing time.

Whole **BROWN LENTILS** (*sabat masoor*), are pink lentils with their skin left on, which makes them heartier. They keep their shape when cooked and result in dishes with a lentil soup consistency.

CHICKPEAS (*channa dal*) are a smaller version of the garbanzo bean. This small, dry, unroasted chickpea comes from the black *channa* variety. They have a low rating on the glycemic index, making them perfect in dal for diabetics.

GREEN MUNG BEANS (*sabat moong dal*), come from the commonly cultivated whole green variety of mung beans. They are used for making dals as well as *khichdi,* a dish that combines rice and lentils and has a consistency that varies from soupy to more robust. Once cooked, they take on a creamy consistency.

PIGEON PEAS (*toor dal*), also known as *arhaar dal,* disintegrate completely when cooked, making for a dish with a smooth consistency. One of the oldest lentil varieties cultivated, they are used widely both in Northern and Southern India.

PINK LENTILS (*malka masoor*), are sometimes referred to as Turkish lentils. Pink dal are quite small and they turn yellow when cooked. Light and easy to digest (and requiring hardly any soaking time), they are my favorite.

RED KIDNEY BEANS (*raj ma*), are, like all beans, an excellent source of protein—especially when combined with rice. *Raj ma chawal,* red beans and rice, is a popular lunch meal. These beans hold their shape when cooked through, and yet lend a creamy texture to the recipe. Due to the length of time required to cook the beans, the slow cooker is a perfect appliance for the task.

YELLOW MUNG BEANS (*pili moong dal*) are the husked, and thus lighter, version of the whole mung bean and probably the most common *dal* used in Indian cooking. Yellow mung beans tend to boil over when cooked in a saucepan. However, this is not a concern when they are cooked in the slow cooker, which maintains a consistent temperature.

TECHNIQUES

Two basic methods of preparing Indian food, *tadka* and *bhunna,* cannot be carried out in a slow cooker, but will be among the preparatory or finishing steps for a number of the recipes in this book. *Tadka* is the tempering of whole spices in hot oil or ghee to bloom the flavor of the spices before they are added to dals or rice or vegetable dishes. It is also the word for the oil-spice mixture itself. *Tadka* is normally added to dals just before serving, and when cooking a dal in the slow cooker, this step can be accomplished in a small skillet. Sometimes a recipe may call for making the *tadka* at the beginning of the cooking process, as there are aromatics such as garlic, ginger, and tomatoes added to the *tadka*; here you will prepare the *tadka* in a skillet before adding to the slow cooker. *Bhunna,* which means "to brown," is the slow and methodical browning of aromatics to form the base of a curry or begin the process of sautéing vegetables.

A third traditional cooking method is a close cousin to using the slow cooker. *Dum pukht* is the slow-cooking method for perfect curries, dals, and vegetables. After one browns the aromatics, vegetables, or meat, the flame is turned down low, the pot is covered tightly, and the dish is set to simmer until it's done. When making a biryani (rice layered with marinated meat), for example, the lid is sealed by stretching a rope of wheat dough around the edges of the lid and pan to seal the steam in the pot.

One nontraditional technique I found very beneficial during the development of these recipes was setting the slow cooker on high heat for 15 minutes to heat the insert. Since many times we are either adding hot water, or tempering spices in hot oil or ghee before adding them to the other ingredients, it makes sense to have the insert heated through in preparation to receive these hot ingredients.

And last but not least is the technique that will help with any new recipe you try: read the recipe through completely before starting to cook it. During my cooking classes, I have found that those who were so eager to get cooking that they didn't read the recipe first would miss a step or omit a spice or other ingredient, resulting in a faulty dish. So read ahead for the best possible results, and enjoy!

cutting up a whole chicken

Indians prefer chicken skinned but left on the bone for many dishes: curries stew for a while, and the bones help keep the poultry moist. As most chickens in India are smaller than American ones, I often use Cornish hens for my curries; the instructions below work for these smaller birds, too.

To cut a whole chicken into six or eight pieces (two each of thighs and legs, and two breasts with or without wings attached), start by pressing the thigh backward away from the body to display the joint that connects the thigh to the body. Cut through the joint with a sharp knife; repeat on the other side. Then sever the legs from the thighs by cutting through the cartilage at the joints. Set these pieces aside.

Insert the tip of the knife through the cavity of the breast and backbone to find the space between the bones; slice through, and pry the backbone away from the breast. Place the whole breast on the cutting board with the exposed bones away from you. Press down on the meat with your left hand, and slice the breast in half, exerting a little pressure on the wishbone. Now you should have two breast halves with the wings attached. If the breast halves are large, you can further cut them into two pieces each, providing for a more uniform size of all the chicken pieces. Cut off the end tip of each wing. You can either leave the wings on or sever them from the breast. (Many do not enjoy the wings; I, however, love them! I skin them and add them to all my chicken dishes.) Save the backbone, wing tips, and wings (if not using), to make chicken stock; it is best to freeze them if not using within a day.

To remove the skin from the chicken, grip each piece using paper towels for traction, and peel and cut the skin away from the meat. Dispose of the used paper towels and the skin.

basics and accompaniments

A typical Indian meal consists of many dishes. Curries or dals are eaten along with either rice or flat breads, and often both. There will often also be a side vegetable and various condiments like raitas (yogurt relishes), chutneys (raw or cooked), or aachars (spicy, pungent, or tart green fruit or vegetable pickles). Many of these cannot be made in a slow cooker, and so the recipes in this chapter mostly use other means of preparation. (In the Chutneys chapter, pages 45–51, there are a few cooked chutney recipes that can be made in a slow cooker.)

In addition to accompaniments, here also are recipes to prepare paneer (fresh cheese) and dahi (yogurt). Garam Masala (page 34), a crucial ingredient in Indian cooking often used in marinades and curries, and sometimes as a garnish, is a combination of spices that are roasted and ground—most Indian cooks will make their own. A simple version (with a variation) is provided here; it is best to make small quantities and keep it in an airtight container so its flavors stay vivid.

BASMATI RICE
chawal

2 cups basmati rice

3 cups warm water

1 teaspoon ghee

Basmati rice is one of the most aromatic long grain rices in the world, and it is the choice of most north Indian cooks. Washing the rice and soaking it before cooking yields the maximum flavor and elongates the rice kernels. The addition of ghee further enhances the flavor of this queen of all rice varieties.

.... MAKES APPROXIMATELY 4 CUPS OF COOKED RICE ....

Pick over the rice, removing any foreign objects. In a bowl, wash the rice in several changes of cold water until the water runs clear. In the saucepan you'll use to cook it, soak the rice in the warm water for at least 20 minutes but no longer than 45 minutes.

Over high heat, bring the rice and water to a full boil, add the ghee, cover, and lower the heat to the lowest point. Simmer gently for 8 minutes. Turn off the heat, remove the lid and cover the top of the rice with a paper towel, then replace the lid. Let it stand for 2 to 3 minutes to steam.

Fluff the rice with a fork and serve while it's still steaming hot.

:::::::: **NOTE** This formula of 1 part rice to 1½ cups water is good for up to 3 cups of rice. Thereafter, as you increase the quantity of rice, the quantity of water in this formula should be decreased by about ⅛ cup (2 tablespoons) for each additional cup of rice. For example, if I were to cook 8 cups of rice I would use 10½ cups of water instead of 12; the yield would be about 16 cups of cooked rice.

WHOLE WHEAT FLAT BREADS
chapattis

2¼ cups whole wheat pastry flour (atta)*

¾ to 1 cup warm water

Melted ghee (optional)

Indian flat breads, or *chapattis*, are also known as *rotis* or *phulkas*. Often brushed with a little ghee for additional flavor, these thin puffed delights of bread are always cooked right before the meal (pictured on page x.) If you need to work in advance, see the Note, below. *Chapattis* are traditionally cooked on a *tava* (pictured on page xii), a slightly concave flat griddle similar to a mexican *comal*. A cast iron pan makes a great substitute.

·· MAKES 16 CHAPATTIS ··

Place 2 cups of the flour in a large mixing bowl and form a well in the center. Pour ¾ cup of the water into the well and mix with one hand, slowly incorporating all the flour into a smooth, firm dough, working in a bit more water as necessary to make it come together. Knead the dough by hand on a clean work surface for about 10 minutes, until it is soft and pliable. Cover with a slightly damp kitchen towel and set aside for at least 30 minutes to rest.

To roll the chapattis, put the remaining ¼ cup of flour in a plate near the work surface. Place a *tava* or heavy griddle over medium heat for 2 to 3 minutes, until heated through. Break pieces off the dough and roll into balls 1 inch in diameter. Working with one ball at a time, flatten each ball into the flour, then roll out on a pastry board until it's 5 to 6 inches in diameter.

Check the *tava* to see if it is hot enough by sprinkling it with a few drops of water. They should instantly sizzle. Place one chapatti on the *tava* and turn over when you see small blisters, about 30 to 40 seconds. Cook for 30 seconds on the other side. To puff the chapatti, remove it from the *tava* and, using tongs, place over an open high flame directly on the burner until it puffs up, about 20 to 30 seconds; turn the chapatti over and repeat the process. The ideal *chapatti* should be a puffed up disk with browned spots on it.

Serve the chapattis hot off the flame, either plain or brushed with melted ghee for additional flavor.

:::::::: **NOTE** To make chapattis up to 4 hours in advance, cook them on the griddle and set them aside to cool. Do not stack them until they are completely cool to the touch. Puff them over the gas flame when you are ready to serve.

YOGURT
dahi

3 cups milk

1 rounded teaspoon plain yogurt, store-bought or a previous homemade batch

Indian households make yogurt each night for the next day, culturing fresh milk with a bit of that day's yogurt. It's easy, and worth it: the taste of homemade yogurt is just that much better. A few helpful hints: the milk should feel warmer than your body temperature—if it is has cooled too much, the culture will not develop; and do not use too much starter or let it set too long as it will be too tart. I prefer to use whole milk, though you can use 2 percent fat milk. Use a good brand of plain yogurt for a starter and thereafter use the yogurt you have cultured to start the process.

.... MAKES 3 CUPS ....

Rinse a 4-quart stainless (or stainless lined) saucepan and while it is still wet, add a few cubes of ice and pour the milk into it. (Using a wet pan helps prevent the formation of a skin on the bottom of the pan during cooking because the heat melts the ice first, tempering the milk before it starts to heat through.)

Over high heat, bring the milk to a full boil without stirring it; beware of its boiling over. Remove the saucepan from the heat and allow the milk to cool in it. When it is still warm to the touch, about 95° to 100°F, pour the milk into a ceramic or glass bowl and stir the yogurt into it. Cover the bowl with a lid or plastic wrap, then wrap it with a few kitchen towels to keep the heat and set it in a dark, warm place overnight or for at least 8 hours.

You will know that the yogurt has cultured when a thin film of whey appears on the top. Refrigerate for at least 4 to 5 hours to set completely. Like store-bought yogurt, homemade yogurt can be kept in the refrigerator for about a week.

:::::::: **NOTE** For a thicker consistency, like Greek yogurt, once the yogurt has set and cooled in the refrigerator for at least 6 hours, drape a thin cotton napkin or kitchen towel in a colander with a bowl under it to catch the whey. Spoon in the desired amount of yogurt and set in the refrigerator to drain for at least 5 to 6 hours or until you get the consistency you like.

CHOPPED SALAD OF TOMATOES, CUCUMBERS, AND RED ONION
kachumber

1 peeled English cucumber

1 firm ripe tomato

½ small red onion, diced small

1 serrano chile, minced (optional)

1 tablespoon finely chopped cilantro

½ teaspoon salt

¼ teaspoon black pepper

Juice of 1 lemon

Kachumber is something like a fresh salsa: it is prepared with raw vegetables and seasoned with lemon juice, salt, and pepper; I like to add raw green chiles as well. As a wonderful salad or relish, *kachumber* adds the extra touch of flavor to both Indian and nonethnic meals.

.... SERVES 4 TO 6 ....

Slice the cucumber in half lengthwise and scrape the seeds out with a teaspoon. Dice the seeded cucumber into small pieces. Cut the tomato in half and squeeze out the seeds. Dice it to the same size as the cucumber.

Toss the cucumber and tomato along with all the other ingredients in a mixing bowl, and adjust salt and lemon juice to taste. The *kachumber* is ready to eat at this point; if not serving right away, refrigerate until ready to use. It is best the day it is made.

::::::::: **NOTES** Many do not like raw onions; you can leave them out, or season them with the lemon juice, salt, and pepper about half an hour ahead of preparing the *kachumber*. This mellows the sharpness of the onion.

::::::::: You can add any other raw ingredient, such as radishes, daikon, and bean sprouts. Sprouts should be blanched in boiling salted water before using, as it helps them soften and absorb the flavors of the salt, pepper, and lemon juice.

CUCUMBER AND YOGURT RAITA
kheere ka raita

3 large cucumbers or
2 English cucumbers, peeled

1 cup plain yogurt,
store-bought or homemade
(page 26)

1 serrano chile, minced

2 teaspoons chopped cilantro

1 teaspoon cumin seeds,
dry roasted and ground
(see page 12)

1 to 1½ tablespoons sugar
(optional)

½ teaspoon salt

¼ teaspoon ground
Indian red chile*

Indians serve plain yogurt with just about every meal. We traditionally make our own (see page 12). Sometimes we flavor it with roasted spices and vegetables, creating a delicious raita. Grated cucumber raita is a wonderful replacement for a salad and cools the palate when served with spicy dishes.

······················· SERVES 6 TO 8 ·······················

Slice the cucumbers in half lengthwise and scrape the seeds out with a teaspoon. Grate the cucumber halves into a small bowl. Using your hands, squeeze all the juice out of the cucumbers. Place the cucumbers in a work bowl. Add the yogurt and the rest of the ingredients and mix thoroughly. Taste and adjust the seasoning as desired for sweetness and heat. Refrigerate for about ½ hour before serving.

MINT CHUTNEY
pudine ki chutney

2 or 3 serrano chiles

1 small onion, quartered

2 small cloves garlic

½ cup cilantro leaves and tender stems

1½ cups tightly packed mint leaves

1 teaspoon cumin seeds,* dry roasted and ground (see page 12)

1 teaspoon ground pomegranate seeds*

¾ teaspoon salt

¼ cup plain yogurt, store-bought or homemade (page 26)

Juice of 1½ to 2 limes

Just about every diner at all three of my restaurants asked for mint chutney when placing their order. Fresh, herbal, and spicy, it is a perfect accompaniment to so many dishes. The traditional way to make it is to pulverize mint with cilantro, chiles, and spices on a grinding stone. Modern conveniences—such as a blender—make it easy to put together at the last minute. I add yogurt to create a tangy dipping sauce.

··· MAKES ABOUT 1 CUP ···

Put the chiles, onion, and garlic in a blender with a little water and puree to a fine paste. Add the cilantro, mint, cumin, pomegranate, salt, yogurt, and lime juice and pulse just to blend in the spices. Taste and adjust for salt, lime, and chile. Transfer to a bowl and refrigerate until ready to serve.

INDIAN FRESH CHEESE
paneer

2 quarts whole milk

1 quart buttermilk

The famous Indian cheese, paneer, is made fresh at home. Like farmer's cheese, paneer's only ingredients are milk and a curdling agent, such as buttermilk, lemon juice, or vinegar. I use buttermilk, as the yield is more and the taste is creamier. Paneer is also available in specialty and Indian grocery stores, but the cheese made at home is much softer and more to my taste. It's easy to make and its uses are varied; try it. This recipe yields ¾ pound; you can make any quantity you want, following the basic proportions of two parts milk to one part buttermilk.

···························· MAKES ABOUT 12 OUNCES ····························

Rinse a 4-quart stainless (or stainless lined) saucepan and while it is still wet, add a few cubes of ice and pour the milk into it. (Using a wet pan with ice helps prevent the formation of a skin on the bottom of the pan during cooking because the heat melts the ice first, tempering the milk before it starts to heat through.) Over high heat, bring the milk to a full boil without stirring it; beware of its boiling over. Remove the saucepan from the heat and pour in the buttermilk, stirring constantly. The solids will separate from the liquid, or whey. Set aside.

Place a colander in a deep mixing bowl. (See step-by-step photos on page 32.) Drape the colander with a fine, clean muslin cloth or double-folded cheesecloth, so that the ends hang over the edges. Pour the curds and whey into the cloth, and, when the whey has drained into the bowl, gather up the ends of the cloth and twist them together firmly to force out excess whey. (Save the whey for use in other dishes—see page 89—or use it to store any extra paneer in the refrigerator. See below.)

Once you've wrung out as much whey as you can, place the tightly wrapped bundle on a slightly convex surface (such as an upside down plate or pan) so that the remaining whey can drip away, and put a second plate or flat pan on top. Weight the plate or pan down with something weighing 2 to 3 pounds (such as the same pot used for boiling the milk, now filled with water; this will also allow the pan to soak, making the cleaning easier). Let the paneer sit for about 30 minutes. The resulting paneer will have a texture similar to a firm farmer's cheese. It can be sliced as needed.

If you're not using all the paneer at the time it's made, cut any remaining paneer into 1-inch cubes and sauté in a teaspoon of oil over high heat just to sear all sides lightly. Refrigerate the sautéed paneer in the reserved whey; it's best to use it within a day or two.

making your own paneer

*Pour the curds and whey into a
muslin-lined colander.*

. . . .

*Twist the cloth firmly to force
out the whey.*

. . . .

Let the bundle drain.

. . . .

*The final texture should
resemble farmer's cheese.*

CLASSIC SPICE BLEND
garam masala

1 teaspoon black peppercorns

1½ teaspoons whole cloves

4 black cardamom pods

8 green cardamom pods

2 (2-inch) pieces cassia

1 tablespoon cumin seeds

1 tablespoon coriander seeds

4 whole dried red árbol chiles

1 star anise

Garam masala is an essential ingredient of the Indian kitchen. A blend of spices the exact composition of which varies from household to household, it lends flavor to many dishes. It is best to blend fresh batches of garam masala every so often; store it in an airtight jar in a cool place. See "Spice Preparation 101," page 12, for further guidance on roasting and grinding spices.

.... MAKES ABOUT ⅓ CUP ....

Roast all the spices in a dry nonstick skillet over high heat, stirring or shaking often to avoid burning. When the cumin seeds turn a deep brown color, transfer the spices to a plate and spread out; set aside to cool completely. Grind the spices in either a blender or a spice grinder until pulverized.

:::::::: **VARIATION** Add ½ teaspoon each of ground nutmeg and mace to the other spices in the grinder.

soups

Prior to the British Raj (which lasted from 1858 to 1947), the Indian kitchen rarely prepared and served soups for lunch or dinner. Upper-class Indian families, such my father's family, adapted to English customs in numerous ways, including food. The passion for eating soup as a starter prompted me to use Indian methods and spices to create a variety of them, and this chapter contains soups inspired by traditional recipes for making dals, *rasams*, and *shorbas*.

Lentils and stock both benefit from long slow cooking, and this combination, along with spices, gives us a delicious and nutritious soup, a natural use of the slow cooker. Indian cooks have been preparing dals, or stewed lentil dishes, for centuries, and lentil soup is quite the rage in the West today, starring in many high-end restaurant menus. So it made sense to me to include Mulligatawny Soup (page 41), a British-influenced dal soup. Chicken soup is a cure-all in many cuisines, and *murghi shorba*—chicken soup with rice, spinach, and tomatoes—is no exception. *Shorba*, derived from an Arabic word, means "gravy." It has a soupy consistency, and has been cooked in India since the invasion by Muslim conquerors from the Middle East as far back as the tenth century. The *murghi shorba* (page 38) in this chapter is from a recipe I created during the Bombay Café days. I have included a recipe for Sindhi chicken (Sautéed Chicken with Green Mango Powder, page 40) as well, as it is a by product of *murghi shorba*.

CHICKEN SOUP WITH RICE, SPINACH, AND TOMATOES

murghi shorba

STOCK

1 (4-to 4½-pound) chicken, skinned and cut up (see page 21)

10 cups water

1 large yellow onion, cut into 6 pieces

8 cloves garlic, coarsely chopped

1 (2-inch) piece fresh ginger, peeled and coarsely chopped

3 serrano chiles, with seeds, cut into 3 pieces each

1 carrot, peeled and cut into 1-inch rounds

1 tomato, quartered

4 whole black cardamom pods

1 (2-inch) piece cassia, broken in half

8 cloves

8 to 10 whole black peppercorns

1½ teaspoons salt

1 cup hot cooked rice

1 large tomato, seeded and diced small

10 to 12 large spinach leaves, julienned

¼ cup chopped cilantro, for garnish

1 serrano chile, minced, for garnish (optional)

1 lemon, cut into 8 wedges, for garnish

One of the more popular dishes we served at the Bombay Café was *murghi shorba*. I wanted to offer a soup beyond lentils, so using the basic method of another popular dish, Sautéed Chicken with Green Mango Powder (page 40), I came up with an Indian version of chicken and rice soup. Like any good chicken soup, it is a wonderful comfort for those ailing with a cold—and the addition of chiles certainly clears your sinuses!

If you are looking to make a stock without the flavors of the whole spices, just leave them out. If using this method for the chicken stock required in the Mulligatawny Soup recipe on page 41, do not add the ginger, chiles, cardamom, cassia, or cloves.

························· SERVES 8 ·························

Before prepping the ingredients, turn the slow cooker on to the high setting for 15 minutes, until the insert is warmed through.

To make the stock, add the backbone and wing tips of the cut up chicken to the heated slow cooker along with the water, onion, garlic, ginger, chiles, carrot, tomato, cardamom, cassia, cloves, peppercorns, and salt. Turn the cooker to low and cook for 4 hours.

Add the rest of the chicken pieces, turn the cooker to high, and continue to cook for another 2 hours.

Transfer the pieces of chicken to a platter. Strain the stock and set aside in a saucepan; keep hot on the stovetop until ready to serve. Shred enough chicken to make 1½ cups; reserve the rest for another use, such as Sautéed Chicken with Green Mango Powder (page 40).

Prepare 8 soup bowls with equal amounts of the rice, tomato, spinach, and shredded chicken. Pour hot stock into the bowls, garnish with cilantro, minced serrano chile, and lemon wedges, and serve.

:::::::: **NOTE** To cook chicken for Sautéed Chicken with Green Mango Powder (page 40), increase the number of chickens to two, weighing about 3 pounds each, skinned and cut into 6 pieces each. Reserve the resulting stock for another use.

SAUTÉED CHICKEN WITH GREEN MANGO POWDER

sindhi chicken

2 (3-pound) chickens,
cut up, skinned, and cooked
(see Note, page 38)

3 tablespoons ghee

3 tablespoons ground coriander

1½ teaspoons ground
Indian red chile*

4 teaspoons green
mango powder*

¼ cup chopped cilantro

This recipe uses the chicken that is cooked when making Chicken Soup with Rice, Spinach, and Tomato (page 38). This dish hails from the Sindh region, thus Sindhi chicken. The tart spice crust created by the use of *amchur*, green mango powder, makes this protein a perfect addition to a meal consisting of chickpea lentils with vegetables or curried black-eyed peas along with basmati rice.

······································· SERVES 6 TO 8 ·······································

If the cooked chicken isn't warm, heat it through before starting. Heat half the ghee in a nonstick skillet on high and, when hot but not sizzling, reduce heat to medium-high. Add half of the coriander and red chile along with half the chicken pieces. Sprinkle 1 teaspoon of the mango powder on the chicken pieces, then turn them over and sprinkle on another teaspoon. Increase the heat to high and sauté on high to coat all sides well, about 1 to 2 minutes per side. Transfer chicken pieces to a serving platter and sprinkle with half the cilantro. Repeat with the remaining ghee, spices, chicken, and cilantro. Serve.

MULLIGATAWNY SOUP
dal aur murghi ka shorba

4 or 5 kari leaves*

1½ teaspoons coriander seeds

1 (1-inch) piece fresh ginger, peeled and coarsely chopped

4 or 5 cloves garlic, coarsely chopped

6 cups chicken stock (page 38) or canned chicken broth

2 tablespoons canola oil

1 small yellow onion, diced small

2 bay leaves

2 teaspoons Madras curry powder*

¼ cups pink lentils,* washed (see page 18)

1¼ teaspoons salt

½ teaspoon ground black pepper

1 large Granny Smith apple, peeled and diced small (optional)

1 stalk celery, diced small (optional)

1 cup cooked long grain rice

1 cup coconut milk

1 cup shredded cooked chicken (see page 38)

Lemon wedges, for garnish

Mulligatawny soup was created in the Indian kitchen during the period when the British ruled India. The Brits requested soup for dinner—heretofore a rarity in the Indian meal. Their Indian cooks translated dal into soup by adding chicken stock and, sometimes, chicken pieces; they often could not resist adding Madras curry spices and coconut milk. Interpretations of mulligatawny soup are as varied as can be; here is one approved by my husband, Franklin, a mulligatawny aficionado. The addition of apples and celery to add sweetness to the soup is an innovation, and it's optional.

························· SERVES 6 TO 8 ·························

Before prepping the ingredients, turn the slow cooker on to the high setting for 15 minutes, until the insert is warmed through.

In a blender, puree the kari leaves, coriander, ginger, and garlic along with ¼ cup of the stock. Set aside. Heat the oil in a skillet on high and sauté the onions until translucent, 3 to 4 minutes. Add the bay leaves and Madras curry powder and sauté for another minute. Place the onion mixture in the heated slow cooker along with the lentils, salt, pepper, the rest of the chicken stock, the apples, and the celery. Cover, reduce the power to low, and cook for 4 hours.

Add the rice and coconut milk and continue to cook on for an additional ½ hour. Add the chicken and keep the cooker on warm for no more than another 30 minutes.

Serve hot with the lemon wedges on the side.

TOMATO LENTIL SOUP
rasam

⅓ cup pigeon peas,* washed

4 large fresh tomatoes, peeled and cut in small dice

1 (½-inch) piece fresh ginger, peeled and minced

1 or 2 serrano chiles, minced

½ teaspoon black pepper

1 teaspoon salt

6 cups hot water

1 tablespoon tamarind paste*

Juice of 1 lemon

TADKA

2 tablespoons canola oil

½ teaspoon brown mustard seeds

6 to 8 kari leaves*

2 tablespoons rasam powder*

Chopped cilantro, for garnish

South Indians eat *rasam,* or tomato broth, as part of their *thali,* a complete meal served on a large steel platter with small bowls. The base of this tart peppery tomato soup is *toor dal,* or pigeon peas, cooked to the point of melting into a smooth texture—perfect for the slow cooker. I serve it with store-bought *pappadums,* crispy disks made from sun-dried lentil dough and often season with cumin or black pepper. Once they are roasted or fried, *pappadums* add crunch to the meal; they can also be enjoyed as a snack with drinks before dinner. *Rasam* spice powder is readily available in Indian grocery stores.

.... SERVES 6 TO 8 ....

Before prepping the ingredients, turn the slow cooker on to the high setting for 15 minutes, until the insert is warmed through. Add the pigeon peas, tomatoes, ginger, chiles, pepper, salt, and water to the heated slow cooker and set on low to cook for 6 hours. Remove the insert from the cooker and add the tamarind paste. Using an immersion blender, blend the soup to a fine puree; set aside.

To make the *tadka,* heat the oil on high in a small skillet, with a lid handy. Tilt the pan to form a pool and carefully add the mustard seeds and kari leaves; cover immediately to avoid splattering. When the sputtering of the seeds subsides, add the *rasam* powder and cook, stirring constantly, for about 2 minutes. Be careful not to burn; reduce the heat if necessary. Reheat the soup in a saucepan if necessary; add the *tadka* to the hot soup, garnish with cilantro, and serve.

:::::::: **NOTE** This recipe can easily be reduced by half for a smaller serving, using just 1½ tablespoons of the lentils, dividing the balance of the ingredients by half, and using a 3½-quart slow cooker.

YOGURT SOUP WITH DAIKON
kadhi aur mooli

TADKA

1½ tablespoons canola oil

Pinch of asafetida*

½ teaspoon mustard seeds

½ teaspoon cumin seeds

1 whole dried red árbol chile, broken

1 (1-inch) piece cassia, broken

2 black cardamom pods

4 cloves

5 or 6 kari leaves*

SOUP

2½ cups plain yogurt, store-bought or homemade (page 26)

5 cups water

3 tablespoons chickpea flour*

⅛ teaspoon turmeric

¼ teaspoon ground Indian red chile*

1½ teaspoons salt

1 tablespoon sugar

1 medium daikon, peeled and cut into thin 1½-inch long sticks

While I was in college, I kept a religious fast with my parents on Mondays. We would break the fast with a light yet delicious vegetarian meal at dinnertime. One of my favorite preparations for this meal was this version of *kadhi*, or Gujarati yogurt curry. I have converted it into a soup that can also be served in a traditional manner with Spiced Rice with Potatoes and Peas (page 117), and Sweet-and-Sour Eggplant (page 88). The advantage of using a slow cooker for this soup is that you do not have to concern yourself with the yogurt separating as it cooks. The addition of thin sticks of daikon gives texture.

······················· SERVES 6 TO 8 ·······················

Before prepping the ingredients, turn the slow cooker on to the high setting for 15 minutes, until the insert is warmed through. To make the tadka, heat the oil on high in a small saucepan, with a lid handy. Tilt the oil to form a pool and add the asafetida and mustard seeds; cover immediately to avoid splattering. When the sputtering of the seeds subsides, add the cumin seeds and then the chile, cassia, cardamom, cloves, and kari leaves. Add to the heated slow cooker insert.

To make the soup, in a bowl, whisk the yogurt with the water. Sift the chickpea flour into it and blend again. Add the turmeric, red chile, salt, and sugar. Mix well and add to the slow cooker. Reduce the heat to low and cook for 5 hours. Add the daikon and continue to cook for another half an hour (no longer, or the daikon will overcook). You can remove the cassia, cardamom, and cloves before serving.

chutneys

Globally, Indian food is associated with chutneys, spiced vegetable or fruit relishes typically used to balance flavors in other dishes. Many chutneys are prepared by blending or pulverizing raw ingredients, such as Mint Chutney (page 29). But some require low-heat cooking for a period of time to blend together the fruits and spices. It is these that are best suited to the slow cooker.

In this chapter, I have given you just a few of my favorites. Date and Tamarind Chutney (page 48) is sweet and sour and can be used as a side to almost any meal. It is also a must in the recipe for Pumpkin with Fennel and Tamarind Chutney (page 95). Many brands of this sweet chutney are available, but there is nothing like the homemade one. Mixed Dried Fruit Chutney (page 47) is a take on *murraba*, a jam-like spiced preserve, and Sweet Tomato Chutney (page 50) is my interpretation of the flavors of Bengal.

These chutneys are versatile: they can be served with all kinds of meals, as a relish for a roast, a spread for sandwiches, or an accompaniment to a cheese platter. Well worth the effort!

gathering around the table

I am fortunate to have known all four of my grandparents. One thing they had in common was spending as much time as they could with family, and Sunday lunches were the pinnacle. My paternal grandmother's menu was always the same: spiced goat with onions and tomatoes (*bhunna ghosht,* see page 75), cauliflower with ginger and cumin (page 80), and whole black lentils (*ma sababth dal,* similar to the recipe on page 106), all accompanied of course by *raita* (page 28), cucumber and tomato salad (*kachumber,* page 27), rice with peas (page 117) and *chappatis* (page 25). My maternal family, which hailed from the province of Sindh, made Sindhi curry (page 40), a lentil stew with a plethora of vegetables, and goat cooked with onion, rum, and saffron (*sel mutton,* see page 59) all accompanied by basmati rice with browned onions (page 115), *rotis* (similar to *chapattis*), and various *achaars* (pickles).

Today, to everyone's delight, we try to have our family lunches with the children and grandchildren whenever possible. And yes, we have as many dishes as I did growing up. The only difference is that after relishing the meal, my husband Franklin and our son-in-law, Fred, used to wish we too had the domestic help that was available to us back in India to deal with the mound of pots and pans one ends up using while making traditional Indian meals. Now that we use a slow cooker or two, Franklin and Fred have fewer dishes to wash!

MIXED DRIED FRUIT CHUTNEY
sukhe phal ki chutney

½ cup apple cider vinegar

½ cup sugar

3 ounces jaggery,*
broken into pieces

2 bay leaves

5 or 6 cloves

1½ teaspoons ground
Indian red chile*

¼ teaspoon turmeric

1 (1-inch piece) fresh ginger,
peeled and cut into thin
julienne

8 ounces dried apricots, cut
into ¼-inch slices

4 ounces dried pears,
cut into ¼-inch slices

4 ounces dried sour cherries

4 ounces dried orange-flavored
cranberries

1½ cups hot water

With the array of dried fruits available here in the United States, I cannot help but make this multipurpose chutney often. I serve it with Roast Chicken à la Rama (page 60) and as a sweet element on a cheese platter. Combine your own mix of dried fruits, total weight 1¼ pounds, depending on what is available in the market.

I used a 3½-quart slow cooker to make this quantity; if you wish to double the recipe, you will need to use a larger capacity slow cooker. I uncover the insert for the last half hour, turning the heat to high to evaporate some of the extra liquid trapped in it.

·· MAKES ABOUT 3¼ CUPS ··

Before prepping the ingredients, turn the slow cooker on to the high setting for 15 minutes, until the insert is warmed through.

Combine all the ingredients in the cooker and mix well; reduce the temperature to low and cook, covered, for 4½ hours. If possible, stir once or twice during that period. Then turn the setting to high and cook uncovered for an additional ½ hour, stirring a few times, to reduce the chutney until it resembles a thick preserve. Remove the bay leaves and cloves, cool the chutney to room temperature, and pour it into clean jars. Refrigerate for up to 2 to 3 months; be careful to avoid contamination by using a clean dry spoon each time you use any and do not return any unused chutney from the dinner table back into a sterilized jar.

DATE AND TAMARIND CHUTNEY
imli ki chutney

1 pound seedless tamarind pulp, preferably half Indian and half Thai (see Note)

6½ cups boiling water

1 pound pitted dates

4 tablespoons roasted ground cumin (see page 12)

Pinch of asafetida*

1 tablespoon freshly ground black pepper

1 tablespoon ground Indian red chile*

4 teaspoons black salt*

2 teaspoons salt

2 cups sugar

8 ounces jaggery,* broken up

This sweet-and-sour traditional chutney has a variety of uses in an Indian kitchen—for example, you will find it being used in Pumpkin with Fennel and Tamarind Chutney (page 95). It's a great accompaniment for Indian snacks, and I love it with all of the rice recipes in this book.

You can find tamarind pulp extracted and bottled as paste at most Indian grocery stores, though I still prefer to process the pulp myself. I use a combination of Indian and Thai tamarind: the Indian is more sour and darker and the Thai is a little sweeter and much pulpier. You can, of course, use whichever is available or convenient. Making a large quantity of this chutney makes sense, as it can hold in the refrigerator for up to a year; you can also halve the recipe. Store the chutney in sterilized jars; be careful to avoid contamination by using a clean dry spoon each time you use any and do not return any unused chutney from the dinner table back into a sterilized jar.

.... MAKES ABOUT 2 QUARTS ....

Break the tamarind pulp into pieces in a large bowl. Pour over 5 cups of the boiling water and leave to soak overnight. In another bowl, pour 1 cup of the boiling water over the dates and allow them to soak overnight.

Before prepping the ingredients, turn the slow cooker on to the high setting for 15 minutes, until the insert is warmed through.

Knead the lumps of soaked tamarind with your fingers. Then force the tamarind pulp and the dates through a fine sieve into another bowl, working ½ cup at a time and scooping out the pulp remaining in the strainer; set this aside in another bowl. When all the tamarind and dates are strained, add the remaining ½ cup of hot water to the pulp in the second bowl and knead it again, then repeat the straining procedure to get the maximum amount of pulp out of the tamarind and dates.

Pour the tamarind-date pulp into the heated slow cooker insert and add all the other ingredients. Stir to mix well. Set the cooker on low for 6 hours; if possible, stir the chutney once or twice after it starts to simmer. Uncover the insert for the last hour of cooking and continue to cook on low heat.

Transfer the chutney to another bowl to cool down to room temperature before pouring into sanitized jars. Store in the refrigerator, tightly capped, for up to a year.

:::::::: **NOTE** You can use 6 cups of tamarind paste, or already strained tamarind pulp, if available, adding ½ cup of hot water before adding it to the cooker (you will still have to soak and strain the dates). Avoid using a dark tamarind paste, as the very concentrated black, tart paste is unsuitable for this recipe.

SWEET TOMATO CHUTNEY
meethi tamatar ki chutney

1 (28-ounce) can whole peeled tomatoes

¼ cup sugar

2 ounces jaggery,* broken into pieces

1 tablespoon canola oil

1 tablespoon panch puran*

8 to 10 kari leaves*

2 serrano chiles, cut into ⅛-inch thick rounds

1½ tablespoons white vinegar

One of the more popular chutneys we served at both the Bombay Café and Neela's was this sweet tomato chutney. Its uses are many—it can be a relish, a sandwich spread, and an accompaniment to many Indian snacks. Or pair it with some of the hearty meat dishes in this book, such as Lamb with Spinach (page 76), *saag gosht*.

Using a smaller 3½-quart slow cooker is better for this recipe, but if you wish to double the quantity, a larger capacity slow cooker would be best.

······································· MAKES ABOUT 2 CUPS ·······································

Before prepping the ingredients, turn the slow cooker on to the high setting for 15 minutes, until the insert is warmed through.

Drain the tomatoes and coarsely chop them in a food processor. Add the chopped tomatoes, sugar, and jaggery to the slow cooker. Heat the oil in a small saucepan on high heat, with a lid handy. Tilt the pan to form a pool and carefully add the *panch puran*, kari leaves, and chiles to the oil; cover immediately to avoid splattering. As soon as they stop sputtering, transfer oil and spices to the slow cooker. Mix well, cover, and cook on low for 2 hours.

Transfer the chutney to a mixing bowl to cool to room temperature. Stir in the vinegar and refrigerate until ready to serve. If you intend to store the chutney for later use, transfer to a sterilized jar, close tightly, and refrigerate for up to 10 days; be careful to avoid contamination by using a clean dry spoon each time you use any and do not return any unused chutney from the dinner table back into a sterilized jar.

curries

When I asked our cook Chandan the definition of the word "curry," he said that the method of browning, *kardho* in Hindi, results in a *kadhi*, which is the northern Indian pronunciation of "curry." With further research, I learned that in the southern Indian language Tamil the word "*kari*" denotes a sauce. Chandan was not wrong, though, as the masalas, or bases, of most curries, especially those from North Indian states, require the *bhunno*, or browning step. The browning of aromatics such as onions, ginger, garlic, and tomatoes, along with spices, results in a rich and delicious masala. Curries prepared in a slow cooker benefit from the slow infusion of these browned masalas. I have adapted traditional methods as necessary to prepare these curries in the slow cooker. For example, I begin by heating the slow cooker insert on the high setting, as the browned spice mixes prepared in a skillet are hot when they go into the cooker.

I encourage you to use the slow cooker, the basic curry masala recipe that launches this chapter (page 54), and your choice of meats to create some delicious one-pot meals.

BASIC CURRY MIX
curry ka masala

⅓ cup canola oil

4 cups minced yellow onions (about 4 or 5 small)

1 (3-inch) piece fresh ginger, peeled and coarsely chopped

12 cloves garlic, coarsely chopped

3 cups pureed fresh tomatoes (about 4 or 5 medium)

2½ tablespoons ground coriander

1½ tablespoons roasted ground cumin (see page 12)

½ teaspoon turmeric

1 to 1½ teaspoons ground Indian red chile*

1 teaspoon salt

Traditionally, meat and poultry are cooked on the bone in curries. These days, for the sake of convenience, we tend to use boneless meat and poultry, and it is for these recipes that this curry base works very well—you'll see it incorporated in a number of recipes in this and other chapters. It can be made in the quantity specified or increased twofold or threefold, as desired (and according to the capacity of your slow cooker) and frozen in freezer bags with the air removed.

It is imperative to sauté the onions until well browned as otherwise there is a residual taste of raw onions. The onions in the United States are large and contain a lot of water; try to use as small a size as you can find.

.... MAKES ABOUT 4 CUPS ....

Before prepping the ingredients, turn the slow cooker on to the high setting for 15 minutes, until the insert is warmed through.

Heat a wide, heavy-bottomed saucepan over high heat, add the oil and fry the onions, stirring often. Once the onions are translucent, after about 5 minutes, turn down the heat to medium-high and sauté for 10 minutes, or until the onions are deeply browned.

Meanwhile, puree the ginger and garlic in a blender, using a little water to get a smooth paste. When the onions are browned, add the ginger-garlic puree, tomatoes, coriander, cumin, turmeric, chile, and salt, mix well, and transfer to the heated slow cooker insert. Pour a cup of water into the hot saucepan and stir and scrape to deglaze the residual spices from the pan; add to the cooker. Set on low and cook for 5 hours. This will keep in the refrigerator for up to a week in a covered container. Alternatively, it can be stored in plastic bags, with all the air removed, in the freezer for up to a month.

BONELESS CHICKEN CURRY
murghi masala

2 cups Basic Curry Mix
(page 54)

1 pound skinless, boneless
chicken thighs, cut into
1½-inch cubes

1 pound skinless, boneless
chicken breasts cut into
1½-inch cubes

1 teaspoon salt

¼ cup chopped cilantro

We served frankies, a favorite Indian roadside snack, at the Bombay Café (see page 56). The customers liked the filling so much that we offered it separately as a curry. Cooking boneless chicken curry in a slow cooker is a challenge, since the masala spice base needs time to develop, and that would be too long for the chicken. I solved the problem by making the base—which works for many other curries too—separately (page 54) and then finishing it like this.

·· SERVES 6 TO 8 ··

If the curry mix has just been cooked and is still hot, add the chicken and salt and cook for 2 hours on low (preheat the slow cooker insert if necessary by turning it to high for 15 minutes before adding the curry masala, chicken, and salt). Stir in the cilantro before serving.

If the curry mix was made earlier and refrigerated, heat it thoroughly in a saucepan over high heat. Meanwhile, preheat the slow cooker insert by turning it to high for 15 minutes. Transfer the heated curry masala to the slow cooker, add the chicken and salt to taste, and cook for 2 hours on low. (Alternatively, you can heat the sauce on the high setting of the slow cooker for 1 hour before adding the chicken.) Stir in the cilantro before serving.

CURRIED CHICKEN FRANKIES
murghi frankies

1 red onion, sliced thin

Juice of 1 lemon

Salt

12 *rotis* or small flour tortillas

About ½ cup canola oil

4 eggs, beaten

Boneless Chicken Curry
(page 55)

1 cup Mint Chutney (page 29)

½ cup Date and Tamarind
Chutney (page 48)

For our Bombay Café frankies—a popular roadside snack in India—we cooked boneless chicken in a traditional curry base (page 54), wrapped it in flour *rotis* (flat breads) with an egg wash on one side, seasoned it with spicy chutneys, and folded the *roti* around the filling like a burrito. If you don't have *rotis*, flour tortillas work fine, too.

·························· SERVES 6 (2 FRANKIES PER PERSON) ··························

Combine the onion, lemon juice, and a pinch of salt in a small bowl and leave to marinate for 10 to 15 minutes before using. If you wish to prepare this in advance, refrigerate the mixture until ready to use.

Heat a skillet on medium-high heat, brush with a little oil, and place a *roti* in it. Brush a tablespoon or so of beaten egg on the top side of the *roti*. As the heat cooks the egg, gently flip the *roti* over. Add drops of oil along the border of the *roti* to finish cooking; this will take less than a minute.

Transfer the *roti* to a cutting board with the egg side down. Spread about 2 tablespoons of chicken curry down the center and add a teaspoon each of the two chutneys and some of the marinated red onions along with a sprinkling of the juice. Fold up one edge of the *roti* over the filling about an inch, then roll the *roti* to encase the filling like a burrito, leaving one end of the *roti* roll open.

BRAISED CHICKEN WITH DRIED FENUGREEK
methi murghi

4 tablespoons canola oil

3 whole black cardamom pods

2 (1-inch) pieces cassia

6 cloves

1 star anise

2 small bay leaves

3 or 4 whole dried red árbol chiles

2 large yellow onions, sliced thin

4 or 5 large cloves garlic, minced

1 (1½-inch) piece fresh ginger, peeled and minced

2 tablespoons ground coriander

1 tablespoon roasted ground cumin (see page 12)

¼ teaspoon turmeric

1 teaspoon ground Indian red chile*

1½ teaspoons salt

1½ tablespoons yogurt, store-bought or homemade (page 26)

½ cup dried fenugreek leaves*

2 large tomatoes, sliced thin

6 bone-in chicken thighs, skinned (see page 21)

6 bone-in chicken legs, skinned (see page 21)

The addition of dried fenugreek leaves to the classic chicken masala lends an earthy flavor that is unsurpassable. I remember that at the end of the meal, my father would ask for a last *chapatti* to be prepared for him. He would then ask the cook to smother it with the last evidence of the masala left in the saucepan. Yum!

I did not think I was going to get the same result as braising in a saucepan—I thought the chicken would lack the flavor derived from browning in the spice mix—but to my delight, the end result was as good as ever. It is important to brown the onions before adding them to the slow cooker for the flavors to develop properly. This recipe uses the legs and thighs of the chicken, as the dark meat can handle the length of time required to get maximum depth of flavor. Should you wish to add chicken breasts, use the ones on the bone and add them to the pot 1½ hours into the cooking, as they take less time to absorb the full masala flavoring.

.... SERVES 6 ....

Heat the slow cooker on high with 1 tablespoon of the oil. After 15 minutes, add the cardamom, cassia, cloves, star anise, bay leaves, and árbol chiles. Meanwhile, heat the remaining 3 tablespoons of oil in a large frying pan over medium-high heat and sauté the onions for 12 to 15 minutes until deep golden brown. Add these to the heated spices in the slow cooker. Add the garlic, ginger, coriander, cumin, turmeric, ground red chile, salt, yogurt, fenugreek, tomatoes, and chicken pieces and stir well to coat all the pieces of chicken in the sauce. Cover and cook for 3½ hours on low heat. Remove the cassia pieces, cardamom, cloves, and bay leaves, and serve.

CORNISH HENS WITH RUM AND SAFFRON
sel murghi

3 tablespoons canola oil

1 teaspoon cumin seeds

2 large yellow onions,
sliced thin

4 cloves garlic, minced

1 (2-inch) piece fresh ginger,
peeled and minced

2 (1-inch) pieces cassia

2 whole black cardamom pods

3 or 4 whole cloves

1 bay leaf

2 tablespoons ground coriander

1 tablespoon roasted
ground cumin (see page 12)

½ teaspoon turmeric

1 teaspoon ground
Indian red chile*

2 fresh tomatoes, diced

2 whole peeled canned
tomatoes, crushed

⅓ cup juice from the
canned tomatoes

⅓ cup plain yogurt,
store-bought or homemade
(page 26)

1½ teaspoons salt

2 serrano chiles, sliced in
half lengthwise

½ cup dark rum

½ teaspoon saffron threads

3 (1½-pound) Cornish hens,
skinned and cut into 8 pieces,
including wings (see page 21)

⅓ cup chopped cilantro

On my many visits to India, I have sat with various members of the family gathering ideas for creating different curries. My mother's aunt told me that it was most important to add rum and saffron to a Sindhi-style meat curry, *sel gosht*, in which meat is cooked for long hours with aromatics and whole and ground spices until the pieces melt in the mouth. I have taken liberties with this recipe to create a flavorful but lighter stew using Cornish hens and the slow cooker.

This recipe is best in a 6-quart slow cooker. It can also be doubled for a larger number of guests or cut in half for just two or three people. If your cooker is oval in shape, it is best to place the Cornish hen pieces in a single layer after mixing with the spice mix. Otherwise, try to spread the pieces throughout the cooker bowl with enough spice mix between the pieces.

.... SERVES 6 TO 8 ....

Before prepping the ingredients, turn the slow cooker on to the high setting for 15 minutes, until the insert is warmed through.

In a skillet, heat the oil over high heat, with a lid handy. Tilt the pan to pool the oil and carefully add the cumin seeds; cover immediately to avoid splattering. When the sputtering subsides, add the sliced onions and brown for about 10 minutes over medium-high heat. Add the garlic, ginger, cassia, cardamom, cloves, and bay leaf to the browned onions and sauté for 1 minute before transferring to the slow cooker.

Set the skillet aside. In the bowl of the cooker, combine the sautéed onions with the ground coriander and cumin, turmeric, red chile, fresh and canned tomatoes, tomato juice, yogurt, salt, serrano chiles, rum, and saffron. Mix well.

Use the saved skillet to sear the hen pieces in batches; place them in the slow cooker and turn them in the spice mix. Arrange them as uniformly as possible. Turn the cooker to low, cover, and cook for 3½ hours. Turn the cooker to warm, and remove the cassia pieces, cardamom, cloves, and bay leaf. Stir in the cilantro when ready to serve.

ROAST CHICKEN À LA RAMA

1 (4- to 5-pound) chicken

½ cup plus 1½ teaspoons kosher or sea salt

1 cup brown sugar

8 cups water; plus ½ cup hot water

6 to 8 whole dried red árbol chiles

5 tablespoons canola or vegetable oil

2 large onions, sliced lengthwise

2 pieces cassia

2 whole black cardamom pods

5 or 6 cloves

6 to 8 whole black peppercorns

2 bay leaves

Growing up, I spent many holiday months at my grandfather's house in Bombay. It was a joint family setup with one kitchen feeding twenty-five to thirty people. Everyone had their favorites and I would look forward to the nights my granduncle would ask Rama, the senior cook, to prepare his famous roast chicken. (Though our kitchens did not have ovens, no one ever thought to ask how he roasted a chicken without one.) Chickens were brought into the family compound live in a basket on the back of a bicycle for my grandfather to choose among. You could not get fresher food.

This recipe is a good translation of Rama's chicken (though I don't know if he brined his as I do mine). Splitting the chicken in half allows for maximum browning and flavor. If you are unable to split the bird, ask the butcher to do it for you. This recipe can only accommodate one chicken: perfect for a family of four! Though if you have two slow cookers, double the recipe and use both: this is a great dish for entertaining.

.... SERVES 4 ....

Cut the chicken in half by removing the backbone and splitting the bird down the breast bone side. Remove any excess fat from the insides of the chicken. The night before roasting the chicken, mix ½ cup of the salt with the brown sugar in 8 cups of water to create a brine. Break half of the red chiles in two and add these to the brine. Place the bird skin side down in a large roasting pan or bowl and pour in the brine. Place a dinner plate on the chicken to submerge it in the brine. Refrigerate overnight.

When ready to cook the chicken, remove it from the brine and pat it dry completely. Let dry for about half an hour to bring to room temperature.

Turn the slow cooker on to the high setting for at least 15 minutes, to warm the insert through. Heat 3 tablespoons of the oil in a large skillet and add the onions. Break the rest of the red chiles in half and add them to the pan. Add the cassia, cardamom, cloves, peppercorns, and bay leaves. Fry the onions over medium-high heat until dark brown, 8 to 10 minutes. Season with 1 teaspoon of the salt, transfer to a plate, and set aside.

Over high heat, add 1 tablespoon of the oil to the skillet and carefully place half of the chicken skin side down in the skillet to brown the skin. The fat and any leftover moisture in the chicken will splatter, so it is best to cover it partially. Once the skin is lightly browned, about 5 minutes, transfer it to the plate with the onions. Pour in the remaining tablespoon of oil and brown the other half of the chicken.

Place the two chicken halves, skin side down, in the slow cooker. If you have an oval shaped one, they should fit perfectly; they might overlap a bit in a round one. Season them with the remaining ½ teaspoon of salt and cover them with the browned onion-spice mix. Add the ½ cup of hot water to the slow cooker. Cook on low for 2 hours. Turn the chicken halves over (so they are now skin side up) and continue to cook for another hour.

Transfer the chicken halves to a warm serving plate. Carefully pour the juices and the onion-spice mix from the slow cooker insert into a saucepan set over medium-high heat and reduce the gravy by half. Pour over the chicken and serve.

TOMATO-BUTTER SAUCE
makhni

6 tablespoons butter

1 cup heavy cream

1 cup half-and-half

¼ teaspoon saffron threads (optional)

2 (28-ounce) cans tomato sauce, preferably without salt

½ cup water

1 (2½-inch) piece fresh ginger, peeled and minced

2 or 3 serrano chiles, minced

1½ teaspoons garam masala, store-bought or homemade (page 34)

2 tablespoons roasted ground cumin (see page 12)

¾ to 1 teaspoon ground Indian red chile*

1¼ teaspoons salt

4 tablespoons sugar

2 tablespoons dried fenugreek leaves*

2 heaping tablespoons chopped cilantro

Chicken tikka masala has become an international phenomenon served in Indian restaurants all over the world; it's so beloved in England that it's sometimes referred to as the national dish! The original recipe, known as butter chicken, came from one of the first tandoori restaurants in Delhi, Moti Mahal. Tandoori chicken pieces were added to tomato-cream sauce and served with naan, tandoor-baked flat bread. (Indian grocers and many specialty stores sell frozen naan.)

Here is the simple yet delicious recipe for the *makhni* (butter sauce). One can then add grilled marinated chicken (page 64) or even just sautéed pieces of boneless chicken, to make chicken tikka masala. For a vegetarian version, use cubes of seared paneer (page 31) or sautéed mushrooms.

.... MAKES 2½ QUARTS ....

Heat the cooker on high and add the butter to melt. This will take about 10 minutes.

Add the cream and half-and-half to the melted butter. Add the saffron and mix well. Add the tomato sauce, then rinse the cans with ¼ cup of water each to get all the sauce; add this to the cooker. Add the ginger, serrano chiles, garam masala, cumin, ground red chile, salt, sugar, and fenugreek, and mix well. Cover, reduce heat to low, and cook 6 hours. When ready to serve, stir in the chopped cilantro.

Cool any unused sauce to room temperature and store for later use—either in sterilized jars for up to 2 weeks in the refrigerator or in plastic bags, with all air removed, in the freezer for up to 3 months.

CHICKEN KABOBS IN GREEN SPICES
mirch masala tikka

8 to 10 cloves garlic,
coarsely chopped

1 (2-inch piece) fresh ginger,
peeled and coarsely chopped

4 serrano chiles,
coarsely chopped

1 bunch cilantro,
tough stems discarded

12 to 15 fresh mint leaves

1 tablespoon garam masala,
store-bought or homemade
(page 34, Variation)

1 tablespoon ground coriander

1 tablespoon roasted
ground cumin (page 12)

½ teaspoon ground
Indian red chile*

2 pounds skinless, boneless
chicken breast and thigh meat,
cut into bite-size pieces

1 teaspoon salt

2 tablespoons canola oil

These delectable morsels of chicken are delicious to serve on their own as an appetizer. With Tomato-Butter Sauce (page 62), they also are the basis of luscious chicken tikka masala (see Notes).

·· SERVES 6 TO 8 ··

Pulse the garlic, ginger, serrano chiles, cilantro, and mint leaves in a blender, using about ¼ cup of water to make into a smooth puree. Transfer to a mixing bowl and stir in the garam masala, coriander, cumin, and ground red chile.

Place the chicken in a large bowl and sprinkle with the salt. Add the marinade and turn the chicken pieces to coat well. Set aside for at least ½ hour at room temperature or up to 6 hours in the refrigerator. Bring the chicken to room temperature before proceeding.

When ready to cook, add the oil to the chicken pieces, stirring to coat well. Thread the pieces onto skewers and barbecue over hot coals or cook under a broiler for 6 to 8 minutes a side.

:::::::: **NOTES** To make chicken tikka masala, add the cooked pieces of chicken to 1½ cups or more of Tomato-Butter Sauce (page 62), heat through, and serve garnished with chopped cilantro.

:::::::: The kabobs can be made in advance; keep refrigerated for up to 2 days. It is easy to reheat them in the sauce itself.

YOGURT AND BLACK PEPPER CHICKEN
dahi aur kali mirch murghi

1 (2½-inch) piece fresh ginger, peeled

10 cloves garlic

1¼ cups plain yogurt, store-bought or homemade (page 26)

¾ cup heavy cream

2 (2½-to 3-pound) chickens or 3 Cornish hens, skinned, boned, and cut into 6 pieces each (see page 21)

6 to 8 whole black peppercorns

1 teaspoon salt

4 serrano chiles, cut lengthwise into 4 pieces each

2 tablespoons ghee

1 tablespoon coarsely crushed black peppercorns

This was a dish that I learned from a cousin and that has since been a favorite of my family. Its gravy is similar to a jus, without the usual curry spices. It can be prepared in advance for later use. The addition of a hot crushed black pepper *tadka* prior to serving adds spice and aroma to the dish. Yogurt needs to be cooked on low heat, as it tends to curdle, thus the slow cooker works very well for this method (I also add cream to the yogurt, which keeps it from breaking completely). Cooking on a low temperature and not having to stir constantly also makes it easy to get smoother gravy.

SERVES 6 TO 8

Cut ½ inch of the ginger into thin matchsticks and set aside. Mince the remaining 2-inch piece of ginger along with the garlic. In a mixing bowl, whisk together the yogurt and cream along with the minced ginger and garlic. Put the chicken pieces along with the yogurt-cream mixture and the whole black peppercorns and salt in the insert of the slow cooker. Mix well and let marinate for 1 hour.

Wipe any marinade from the sides of the insert above the poultry with a wet paper towel, as it will burn. Cook on low heat for 3½ hours. When the timer sounds and the slow cooker turns to warm, stir in the sliced ginger and chiles and re-cover the cooker. If not using within the hour, shut the power off; you can warm the dish through in a saucepan if needed.

When ready to serve, transfer to a serving bowl. In a small skillet or saucepan over high heat, heat the ghee, add the crushed black peppercorns, and immediately pour over the chicken.

KERALA FISH CURRY
meen moili

MASALA PASTE

3 cloves garlic, minced into a paste

½ teaspoon ground cloves

1 teaspoon ground cinnamon

2 teaspoons ground fennel seeds

2 teaspoons ground Indian red chile*

2 tablespoons ground coriander

1 teaspoon ground black pepper

1½ teaspoons salt

½ cup water

1 tablespoon oil

2 medium onions, sliced thin

2 or 3 serrano chiles, sliced thin

1 (1-inch) piece fresh ginger, peeled and julienned

10 to 12 kari leaves*

2 (15-ounce) cans coconut milk

½ cup water

There are many recipes for *meen moili*, a fish curry from the southern state of Kerala. I got this one from a well-known South Indian chef many years ago, and it has remained my go-to South Indian fish curry. Steamed basmati rice (page 24) and Green Beans with Mustard Seeds and Onions (page 84), are perfect accompaniments.

If cooked over too high a heat, coconut milk tends to separate, so the benefit of the slow cooker is that it allows you to use coconut milk with ease. Here, simmering the milk with spices results in a luscious sauce. This dish is perfect for entertaining, as you can keep the curry warm in the cooker while adding sautéed pieces of fish, and they will hold without overcooking or falling apart. Shrimp is a great alternative, too (see Note, page 68).

·· SERVES 6 TO 8 ··

Before prepping the ingredients, turn the slow cooker on to the high setting for 15 minutes, until the insert is warmed through.

In a bowl, mix the ingredients for the masala paste until combined then set aside.

Heat the tablespoon of oil in a skillet over high heat. Add the onions, chiles, ginger, and kari leaves and fry for 2 minutes, until the onions are just soft. Transfer to the slow cooker insert. Add the masala paste and stir in the coconut milk, rinsing each can with ¼ cup of water and adding this to the slow cooker. Cook for 2½ hours on low. This curry can be made ahead of time to this point and either kept on the warm setting for up to an hour or cooled and then reheated quickly in a saucepan when you want to continue with the next step.

ingredients and method continued
::

FISH

1½ pounds mild white fish fillets, such as red snapper, tilapia, or thin fillets of halibut

Juice of 2 lemons

1 teaspoon turmeric

½ teaspoon salt

2 to 3 tablespoons canola oil

Lemon wedges, for garnish

Trim and cut the fish into 2-inch pieces. In a bowl, combine the lemon juice, turmeric, and salt and mix in the fish to coat well. Let stand for 20 minutes.

Drain the marinade from the fish. Heat the oil in a skillet over medium-high heat and, working a few pieces at a time so as not to overcrowd the pan, fry the fish for 1 to 2 minutes on each side, until the edges are lightly browned. Transfer the fish with a slotted spoon to a paper towel–lined plate and set aside. Once all the fish is sautéed, carefully transfer the pieces to the hot curry and simmer for another minute or more, depending on the thickness of the fish. Serve hot, garnished with lemon wedges.

NOTE If using shrimp, allow for five or six size 16/20 shrimp per person. Peel and devein the shrimp before using. Sauté the shrimp in a skillet over high heat with 1 tablespoon oil for a few minutes, just until they become opaque, before adding to the curry. Be careful not to overcook them, as they will get rubbery.

VARIATION For a vegetarian version of this curry, serve with corn on the cob cut into 1½-inch pieces. Boil the corn until tender, about 3 to 4 minutes, and then add to the curry. Bring the curry to a quick boil and serve. Allow for 2 or 3 pieces of corn per person.

FISH WITH SAUTÉED ONION SAUCE
machchi bassar

5 tablespoons canola oil

1 heaping teaspoon cumin seeds

2 large yellow onions, thinly sliced

2 medium tomatoes, halved and sliced thin

1 (1-inch) piece fresh ginger, peeled and julienned

2 or 3 serrano chiles, sliced thin lengthwise

2 teaspoons ground coriander

½ to 1 teaspoon ground Indian red chile*

¼ teaspoon turmeric

Salt

1½ to 2 pounds skinless mild white fish fillets, such as red snapper, halibut, or tilapia

Chopped cilantro, for garnish

Visits to various family members' homes influenced my cooking as it developed. *Bassar* was a common descriptor for many of the dishes being served: loosely translated, it denotes lots of onions. Here, I have taken that to heart and created a sauce that is perfect for pairing with grilled fish or shrimp, or paneer for a vegetarian version—see the Notes, below. This sauce is easy to double or triple, then freeze in small batches for later use.

.... SERVES 6 TO 8 PEOPLE ....

Before prepping the ingredients, turn the slow cooker on to the high setting for 15 minutes, until the insert is warmed through.

Heat 3 tablespoons of the oil in a skillet on high heat, with a lid handy. Tilt the pan to form a pool and carefully add the cumin seeds; cover immediately to avoid splattering. When the sputtering of the seeds subsides, transfer them and the oil to the heated cooker. Add the onions, tomatoes, ginger, serrano chiles, coriander, ground red chile, turmeric, and 1 teaspoon of salt and stir in ⅓ cup to ½ cup of hot water, depending on how thick you want the sauce to be. Cover and cook on high for 3 hours. Turn the cooker to warm while you sauté the fish.

Heat a large nonstick skillet with the remaining 2 tablespoons of canola oil. Season the fish fillets with salt. When the oil is hot, carefully sear the fish fillets on each side for 2 to 3 minutes depending on the thickness of the fish. Add the fish to the warm sauce and let it simmer to infuse the flavors for 5 minutes. Garnish with chopped cilantro and serve.

:::::::: **VARIATIONS** To serve with shrimp, clean and devein 1½ to 2 pounds of large (16/20) shrimp. Sauté them in the oil for 2 to 3 minutes and then add to the warm sauce and continue to cook on warm for another 5 minutes. Do not overcook. Garnish with cilantro.

:::::::: To serve with paneer, cube ¾ pound of paneer (page 31) and sear it on all sides in the canola oil. Add to the warm the sauce and keep cooking on warm for 10 minutes; garnish with cilantro.

PORK VINDALOO

1 (3½-inch) piece fresh ginger, peeled

3 tablespoons canola oil

½ teaspoon fenugreek seeds*

3 medium yellow onions, thinly sliced

4 pounds pork shoulder, cut into 1½-to 2-inch cubes

10 to 12 cloves garlic, minced

3 to 6 serrano chiles, minced

½ teaspoon turmeric

1½ to 2½ teaspoons ground Indian red chile*

1½ teaspoons salt

2 tablespoons coriander seeds

1 teaspoon cumin seeds

½ teaspoon brown mustard seeds

4 to 6 cloves

3 to 4 black cardamom pods

20 black peppercorns

1 (1-inch) piece cassia

1 teaspoon sugar

2 tablespoons tamarind paste* (see Note)

1 tablespoon white vinegar

Until as late as 1962, the Portuguese ruled the southern Indian state of Goa. *Carne de vinha d'alhos*, a Portuguese dish made with pork, was the basis of the now famous vindaloo served in Indian restaurants. Although many make it with lamb, chicken, or shrimp, I prefer the original recipe with pork, redolent of tamarind, vinegar, and black pepper. Vindaloo is famed for being extremely spicy; adjust the amount of chile, both green and red, to your taste.

·················· SERVES 6 TO 8 ··················

Before prepping the ingredients, turn the slow cooker on to the high setting for 15 minutes, until the insert is warmed through. Julienne 1 inch of the ginger and set aside for garnish. Mince the remaining ginger.

Heat the oil in a large skillet over high heat, with a lid handy. Tilt the skillet to pool the oil and add the fenugreek seeds; cover immediately to prevent splattering. When the seeds have stopped sputtering, add the onions. Sauté the onions for 7 to 8 minutes until light golden brown. Add the browned onions to the slow cooker and mix in the pork, minced ginger, garlic, serrano chiles, turmeric, ground red chile, and salt. Cook on low heat for 3½ hours.

Grind together the coriander seeds, cumin seeds, mustard seeds, cloves, cardamom, peppercorns, cassia, and sugar in a spice grinder. Add the ground spice blend to the pork, mix well, and continue to cook on low for an additional 30 minutes. Turn the slow cooker off and stir in the tamarind pulp and vinegar. Serve garnished with the julienned ginger.

:::::::: **NOTE** If you have bulk tamarind pulp, use a 2-to 3-ounce piece to extract the paste (see page 14).

LAMB CHOPS WITH BROWNED ONIONS AND TOMATOES
masaledar champas

8 cloves garlic, minced

1 (2-inch) piece fresh ginger, peeled and minced

2 teaspoons garam masala, store-bought or homemade (page 34)

2 teaspoons ground fennel seeds

1 teaspoon salt

½ cup plain yogurt, store-bought or homemade (page 26)

9 (1½-inch-thick) sirloin lamb chops (about 3 pounds)

CURRY

3 tablespoons canola oil

4 small yellow onions, sliced thin

2 tablespoons ground coriander

1 tablespoon roasted ground cumin (see page 12)

1 to 2 teaspoons ground Indian red chile*

½ teaspoon turmeric

2 or 3 small bay leaves

1½ teaspoons salt

2 small fresh tomatoes

2 canned whole tomatoes

3 or 4 serrano chiles, halved lengthwise

¼ cup chopped cilantro

Every visit home to India, I ate goat chops cooked in several different styles. In my opinion my aunt's cook made the best *masaledar champas*, tender and redolent with the flavor of all the freshly ground fennel seeds, garam masala, browned onions, and tomatoes. I would scrape up the last of the masala and bits of meat on the plate with a hot chapatti, licking my fingers for every last smidgen of it.

Sirloin Lamb chops are more substantial than rib or blade chops, but both can be used in this recipe. Keep in mind that the slow cooker breaks down the meat quickly, in 3 hours or less on high, or if desired you can cook this recipe on low for 5 hours. Marinating the lamb chops overnight infuses flavor into the meat, but this step can also be cut down to a couple of hours if you are short on time.

··· SERVES 6 ···

Mix the garlic, ginger, garam masala, fennel, and salt with the yogurt. Spread some of this marinade on both sides of each chop. Place the chops in a mixing bowl along with any leftover marinade, cover with plastic wrap, and refrigerate overnight or for at least 2 hours.

Before prepping the remaining ingredients, turn the slow cooker on to the high setting for 15 minutes, until the insert is warmed through.

continued
··················

Heat 2 tablespoons of the oil in a large skillet over high heat. Add the sliced onions and fry, stirring often, for 10 to 12 minutes, until the onions are golden brown. Transfer to the slow cooker insert. Heat the remaining tablespoon of oil in the same skillet. Sear the chops for 3 to 4 minutes on each side and add to the cooker. Mix to spread the browned onions all around the chops. Add the coriander, cumin, red chile, turmeric, bay leaves, and salt. Puree the tomatoes and add to the cooker. Gently turn the chops to coat evenly in the sauce. Add the green chiles, cover, and cook on high for 3 hours, turning the chops over about halfway through the cooking time.

Remove the cover and test the chops for doneness; they should be fork tender and practically falling off the bone. Transfer the chops to a serving platter. Pour the sauce from the cooker into a saucepan. Over high heat reduce the sauce by a third. Remove the bay leaves and place the chops in the saucepan to coat with the reduced sauce. Garnish with cilantro and serve.

:::::::: **VARIATION** You can substitute 1½ cups of Basic Curry Mix (page 54) for the mixture of onions, ginger, garlic, tomatoes, coriander, cumin, red chile, and turmeric. Heat thoroughly before adding the marinated chops.

BROWNED LAMB WITH ONIONS, TOMATOES, AND SPICES

bhunna gosht

6 or 7 cloves garlic, coarsely chopped

1 (2-inch) piece fresh ginger, peeled and coarsely chopped

⅓ cup canola oil

4 small onions, chopped fine

1½ pounds lamb leg meat, cut into 1½-inch cubes

2 or 3 black cardamom pods

2 (1-inch) pieces cassia

5 or 6 cloves

5 or 6 black peppercorns

2 small bay leaves

2 tablespoons ground coriander

1 tablespoon roasted ground cumin (see page 12)

1½ teaspoons ground Indian red chile*

½ teaspoon turmeric

4 medium tomatoes, chopped

1½ teaspoons salt

Chopped cilantro, for garnish

My father's family came from the Punjab region of India, which is now in Pakistan and is known for its meat-rich cuisine. My grandmother's Sunday lunch always included this recipe, served with spiced basmati rice, *bhuga chawal* (page 115), which I recommend, along with sautéed cauliflower, *gobi sabzi* (page 80), as accompaniments.

Lamb takes time to cook and we Indians prefer the meat to fall apart—again, this makes it a good candidate for the slow cooker. I recommend buying leg of lamb cut into cubes or shoulder cuts ready for stew. Lamb is less fatty than young goat, the meat of choice in India. There is a growing market for goat meat in the United States, and if you can get leg meat from the goat, have the butcher clean it and cube it for you and try it in this dish.

·· SERVES 6 TO 8 ··

Before prepping the ingredients, turn the slow cooker on to the high setting for 15 minutes, until the insert is warmed through.

Puree the garlic and ginger in a blender, using a little water to get a smooth paste. Set aside. Heat the oil in a large skillet over high heat and sauté the onions until dark golden brown, about 10 to 12 minutes. Add the garlic and ginger paste to the browned onions and mix well, then add the lamb cubes and sear on all sides. Transfer the meat and sautéed onions to the heated cooker and add the cardamom, cassia, cloves, peppercorns, bay leaves, coriander, cumin, chile, turmeric, tomato, and salt. Mix thoroughly and cook on low for 6 hours.

Remove the cardamom, cassia pieces, cloves, and bay leaves. Garnish with cilantro and serve.

LAMB WITH SPINACH
saag gosht

1 (2-inch) piece fresh ginger, peeled and coarsely chopped

5 or 6 cloves garlic, coarsely chopped

2 medium tomatoes, quartered

1 pound frozen chopped spinach, defrosted

4 tablespoons canola oil

4 small yellow onions, diced small

2 tablespoons chickpea flour*

1½ pounds lamb leg meat, cut in 1½-inch cubes

2 or 3 (½-inch) pieces cassia

6 cloves

6 whole black peppercorns

2 or 3 whole black cardamom pods

2 whole bay leaves

3 tablespoons ground coriander

2 teaspoons roasted ground cumin (see page 12)

1 to 1½ teaspoons ground Indian red chile*

½ teaspoon turmeric

½ cup plain yogurt, store-bought or homemade (page 26)

½ cup dried fenugreek leaves*

2 or 3 serrano chiles, halved lengthwise

1½ teaspoons salt

1 (1-inch) piece fresh ginger, peeled and julienned, for garnish

My father always favored his meat dishes, and this particular one was often served in our home. He relished it with fresh *chapattis* (page 25) and Eggplant with Potatoes (page 85). Add basmati rice (page 24) and you have a meal for a dinner party! If timed properly, this dish, once cooked through, can be served directly from the slow cooker; simply keep it on the warm setting (the beauty of the slow cooker is that the meat won't end up overcooked).

SERVES 6 TO 8

Before prepping the ingredients, turn the slow cooker on to the high setting for 15 minutes, until the insert is warmed through.

Puree the ginger, garlic, and tomatoes in a blender, using a little water to get a smooth paste, and transfer to the slow cooker. In the same blender jar, puree the thawed spinach, using a little water to assist, and add to the cooker.

Heat 3 tablespoons of the oil over high heat in a skillet; add the onions and fry. Turn the heat down to medium-high, stir frequently, and sauté until the onions are a deep golden brown, about 10 to 12 minutes. Add the chickpea flour and stir to brown it and remove the raw taste. Use a little water to make a roux. Add this to the cooker, using a little more water to deglaze the pan and get all the granules of the roux out.

In the same pan, heat the remaining tablespoon of oil and add the lamb pieces in two batches, searing the meat before transferring it to the cooker. Add the cassia, cloves, peppercorns, cardamom, bay leaves, coriander, cumin, ground red chile, turmeric, yogurt, fenugreek, serrano chiles, and salt, mix well, and cook on low for 8 hours. Remove the cardamom, cassia pieces, cloves, and bay leaves. Garnish with the julienned ginger and serve hot.

GROUND MEAT WITH POTATOES AND PEAS
keema aloo mattar

3 small yellow onions, peeled

1 (2-inch) piece fresh ginger, peeled and coarsely chopped

6 cloves garlic, coarsely chopped

2 medium tomatoes, quartered

4 whole peeled canned tomatoes

3 tablespoons canola oil

3 whole black cardamom pods

2 (1-inch) pieces cassia

4 or 5 whole cloves

2 bay leaves

4 or 5 whole black peppercorns

2 pounds 90 percent lean ground beef, or ground lamb or turkey

3 tablespoons ground coriander

2 teaspoons roasted ground cumin (see page 12)

1 teaspoon ground Indian red chile*

¼ teaspoon turmeric

½ teaspoon ground green cardamom pods (see Notes)

1½ teaspoons salt

2 serrano chiles, halved lengthwise (optional)

2 red potatoes, peeled and cut into 1-inch cubes

8 ounces frozen green peas

¼ cup chopped cilantro, for garnish

One of the first dishes that I learned to cook was *keema mattar*. It was the first curry I served my husband, Franklin, and it became a standard at least once a week in our home. *Keema*, or ground meat, is absolute comfort food for an Indian. You can use ground beef, ground lamb, or even ground turkey for this recipe. I have added potatoes to this traditional dish to make it a one-dish meal. Rice or flat breads are perfect accompaniments, and a crisp salad rounds off the meal.

·············· SERVES 6 TO 8 ··············

Before prepping the ingredients, turn the slow cooker on to the high setting for 15 minutes, until the insert is warmed through.

Mince the onions in a food processor or by hand, transfer to a small bowl, and set aside. Puree the ginger and garlic in a blender with a little water to get a smooth paste; transfer to a small bowl and set aside. In the same blender jar, puree the fresh and canned tomatoes along with about 2 tablespoons of the juice from the canned tomatoes.

Heat the oil in a skillet on high heat and sauté the minced onions until golden brown, about 10 to 12 minutes, stirring often. Place the browned onions in the slow cooker insert and add the pureed garlic and ginger mixture and the black cardamom, cassia, cloves, bay leaves, and peppercorns.

Brown the ground meat in the same skillet used for the onions, mashing the meat with a wooden spoon to break it up. Transfer to the cooker insert along with the pureed tomatoes, coriander, cumin, ground red chile, turmeric, green cardamom, salt, serrano chiles, potatoes, and peas. Mix well. Turn the setting to low and cook for 2½ hours. Remove the bay leaves, garnish with the cilantro, and serve.

::::::::: **VARIATION** You can substitute 1½ cups of Basic Curry Mix (page 54) for the mixture of onions, ginger, garlic, tomatoes, coriander, cumin, red chile, and turmeric. Heat thoroughly before adding the green cardamom, salt, serrano chiles, meat, potatoes, and peas.

::::::::: **NOTE** To prepare the green cardamom, split open 20 to 25 green cardamom pods, remove the seeds, and discard the husks. Pulverize in a mortar and pestle. Use the recommended amount and store the rest for future use.

vegetables

India's population is mostly vegetarian, and the variety of vegetables and vegetable dishes is tremendous. From region to region and from home to home, vegetables are prepared in so many different ways that I do not believe I have tasted them all. If variety is the spice of life, then this is the place to be!

This chapter proved to be the most challenging to adapt to slow cooking, as many traditional Indian vegetable recipes start by stir-frying the vegetables with the aromatics and spices, then finishing the cooking process by covering and steaming for just a few minutes. This results in firm yet thoroughly cooked veggies. I found those vegetables cooked in gravy were more suitable for the slow cooker. And the result was as good as if I'd toiled over a saucepan, if not better. These included Curried Peas and Indian Cheese (page 89), Pureed Spinach with Indian Cheese (page 92), and Potatoes and Peas in Tomato Sauce (page 94).

Eggplants shine in the slow cooker: traditionally, cooking techniques for eggplants require a fair amount of oil and moisture to soften the flesh. The slow cooker requires less oil, and the covered pot keeps the moisture in. With the variety of eggplants available in India, I have given you three recipes to enjoy.

Preparations such as Cauliflower with Ginger and Cumin (page 80) and Green Beans with Mustard Seeds and Onions (page 84) proved to be a little more challenging. But by adding tomatoes or onions, I was able to find my way to wonderful renditions of classic Indian stand-alone vegetables. Note that these dishes should not be kept too long on the warm setting, as the residual heat continues to cook them further, taking them past the point of optimal doneness.

CAULIFLOWER WITH GINGER AND CUMIN
gobi sabzi

1 head cauliflower
(about 3 pounds)

3 tablespoons canola oil

1 teaspoon cumin seeds

2 serrano chiles,
cut in 3 pieces each

1 (1-inch) piece fresh ginger,
peeled and cut in thin julienne

1 tablespoon ground coriander

½ to ¾ teaspoon ground
Indian red chile*

½ teaspoon turmeric

1 heaping teaspoon salt

1 medium tomato, diced

Chopped cilantro, for garnish

One of the first vegetables I learned to cook from my aunt Vrinda was *gobi sabzi*, sautéed cauliflower. My family loves it so much that we cook it at least once a week. Try leftovers cold between two slices of toast with a slice of havarti cheese: it's a perfect snack for a picnic or a long drive.

Cauliflower needs to be browned on low heat to help caramelize its sugar and bring out its natural flavor; it's traditionally cooked in a *karahi* or Indian wok. My version here adds tomatoes, then stir-fries the vegetables in a skillet on high heat at the time of serving, reducing the moisture and at the same time browning the cauliflower.

.... SERVES 6 ....

Before prepping the ingredients, turn the slow cooker on to the high setting for 15 minutes, until the insert is warmed through.

Cut the cauliflower into bite-size florets. Use the peeled and diced core and young leaves, too. Heat the oil in a small skillet on high heat, with a lid handy. Tilt the pan to form a pool and carefully add the cumin seeds; cover immediately to avoid splattering. When they finish sputtering, transfer to the heated insert of the slow cooker.

Add the serrano chiles, ginger, coriander, ground red chile, turmeric, salt, and tomato, and mix well. Cook on low for 3 hours. If possible, stir once or twice. The cauliflower should still be firm to the touch.

When ready to serve, transfer the cauliflower with all the juices to a large skillet or sauté pan on high heat and stir-fry until the moisture has been completely absorbed or evaporated. Garnish with cilantro and serve.

KASHMIRI POTATO CURRY
dum aloo

PASTE

1 large onion, coarsely chopped

6 cloves garlic, coarsely chopped

1 (2-inch) piece fresh ginger, peeled and coarsely chopped

2 medium fresh tomatoes

2 whole peeled canned tomatoes

6 black peppercorns

1 teaspoon white poppy seeds (see headnote)

1 tablespoon coriander seeds

1 teaspoon cumin seeds

2 whole dried red árbol chiles

1 teaspoon turmeric

1/8 teaspoon ground mace

1/8 teaspoon ground nutmeg

CURRY

32 walnut-size Yukon gold potatoes, peeled

3 tablespoons canola oil

2 black cardamom pods

4 green cardamom pods

4 to 6 whole black peppercorns

2 (1-inch) pieces cassia

2 bay leaves

4 or 5 whole cloves

1/2 cup plain yogurt, store-bought or homemade (page 26), blended with 1/2 cup water

1 teaspoon ground Indian red chile*

1 1/2 teaspoons salt

1/2 cup chopped cilantro, for garnish

The traditional Kashmiri *dum aloo* calls for deep-frying small potatoes, piercing them with spices, and then stewing them in a tomato-yogurt curry sauce. Due to the ease of the slow cooker, I decided not to deep-fry the potatoes but did prick them with the tip of a sharp knife to infuse the flavors of the sauce into the meat of the potatoes. The flavors penetrated extremely well, yielding a lighter version of the ever-so-delicious *dum aloo*. Tart white poppy seeds (*khuskhus*), help thicken the spice paste; they can be found in Indian grocery stores.

························ SERVES 6 TO 8 ························

Before prepping the ingredients, turn the slow cooker on to the high setting for 15 minutes, until the insert is warmed through.

Puree all the ingredients for the paste in a blender and pour it into the heated slow cooker insert. Use 1/4 cup of warm water to rinse the remaining spice puree from the blender and pour this into the insert.

Using the tip of a sharp knife, prick the potatoes in several places and add to the insert with the oil, black and green cardamom, peppercorns, cassia, bay, cloves, yogurt-water mixture, chile, and salt; mix well. Cover and cook on high for 6 hours.

Remove the black cardamom, cassia pieces, cloves, and bay leaves. Garnish with the cilantro and serve.

GREEN BEANS WITH MUSTARD SEEDS AND ONION
sem bhajji

3 tablespoons canola oil

1 small yellow onion, diced small

6 to 8 kari leaves*

3 or 4 whole dried red árbol chiles, broken in two

1 teaspoon brown mustard seeds

1½ pounds trimmed green beans, cut in ¼-inch pieces

Chopped cilantro, for garnish

Green beans, or French beans as they are known in India, are cooked in very simple ways—just a little heat from chiles, some pungent mustard seeds or earthy cumin seeds, sometimes kari leaves, and the beans. Most recipes in the slow cooker require some kind of moisture; adding onions to the green beans solves the problem of obtaining moisture without any water or stock. The end result is a vegetable dish without gravy, a perfect addition to any meal.

SERVES 6 TO 8

Before prepping the ingredients, turn the slow cooker on to the high setting for 15 minutes, until the insert is warmed through. When it's heated, add 1 tablespoon of the oil to the insert. After a minute, add the onion, kari leaves, and red chiles.

Heat the remaining 2 tablespoons of oil in a small skillet on high heat, with a lid handy. Carefully add the mustard seeds; cover while they sizzle. When the seeds stop sputtering, add them and the oil to the cooker. Add the green beans and salt. Mix well and cook on low for 2 hours. If possible, stir once or twice. Garnish with the cilantro and serve.

EGGPLANT WITH POTATOES
baingan aloo ki sabzi

3 tablespoons canola oil

1 teaspoon cumin seeds

1 (1½-inch) piece fresh ginger, peeled and minced

1 or 2 serrano chiles, chopped

2 large tomatoes, chopped

1½ tablespoons ground coriander

½ to 1 teaspoon ground Indian red chile*

¼ teaspoon turmeric

1 heaping teaspoon green mango powder*

1½ teaspoons salt

3 large Japanese eggplants, or 1 large eggplant (about 1 pound)

3 medium red potatoes

Chopped cilantro, for garnish

Eggplants are indigenous to India, and come in many sizes and shapes, from the large globe to the tiny; from the deep purple to the lilac variegated. Throughout India they are cooked in different ways; one of the common ways is to combine them with potatoes, tomatoes, and spices creating a luscious and hearty vegetable dish. The slow cooker does well with this dish as the potatoes and eggplants cook at the same rate.

·· SERVES 6 TO 8 ··

Before prepping the ingredients, turn the slow cooker on to the high setting for 15 minutes, until the insert is warmed through.

Heat the oil in a small skillet on high heat, with a lid handy. Tilt the skillet to pool the oil and carefully add the cumin seeds; cover immediately to prevent splattering. When they stop sputtering, tip oil and seeds into the heated slow cooker insert. Add the ginger, serrano chiles, tomatoes, coriander, ground red chile, turmeric, mango powder, and salt. Mix well, cover, and cook on high while you prep the eggplant and potatoes.

If using Japanese eggplants, cut into 1½-inch rounds, skin on. If using a globe eggplant, cut into 1½-inch cubes with the skin on; place in water to cover. Peel and cut the potatoes into 8 wedges each and add to the soaking eggplants. After 20 minutes, drain the potatoes and eggplant and add to the slow cooker. Stir to mix well, reduce to low, cover, and cook for 3½ hours. Garnish with cilantro and serve hot.

EGGPLANT WITH YOGURT AND SAFFRON
kashmiri baingan

2 pounds small Indian eggplants (about 18, see Note)

10 to 12 threads saffron

1 tablespoon warm milk

1 tablespoon ground coriander

½ teaspoon ground Indian red chile*

1½ teaspoons salt

⅓ cup corn oil

2 whole black cardamom pods

2 (1-inch) sticks cassia

5 or 6 whole cloves

2 small bay leaves

5 or 6 whole black peppercorns

1 (½-inch) piece fresh ginger, peeled and minced

1 medium yellow onion, sliced thin

¼ cup plain yogurt, store-bought or homemade (page 26)

Chopped cilantro leaves, for garnish

While we were vacationing at Dal Lake, Kashmir, the staff of the houseboat served us their specialties. I remember this one in particular, as it was the first time I had tasted the combination of eggplant, yogurt, and saffron. As saffron grows in Kashmir, is used widely in their food, and often with yogurt as its medium. The eggplants used in this recipe can be purchased from Indian markets or specialty stores. They look like baby versions of large globe eggplants; choose the larger of those available. Though there is a little bit of work required prior to cooking this dish, the result is well worth it.

·········· SERVES 6 ··········

Trim the tough ends of the eggplant stems, leaving the caps intact. Make a crosswise slit halfway through each eggplant from the blossom end. Soak them in water to cover for at least half an hour to open the slits and remove any bitterness.

Before continuing to prep the ingredients, turn the slow cooker on to the high setting for 15 minutes, until the insert is warmed through.

In a small bowl, soak the saffron threads in the warm milk and set aside. In another small bowl, combine the coriander, ground red chile, and ½ teaspoon of the salt.

Drain the eggplants in a colander. Working over a plate, pry open the slits with your fingers and press about ¼ teaspoon of the spice mixture into each eggplant, letting any excess fall onto the plate, and push the slit closed to distribute the spices evenly.

Heat the oil in a large skillet on high heat. Add the cardamom, cassia, cloves, bay leaves, and peppercorns and fry until they sizzle, about 30 seconds. Add the ginger and onions and continue to sauté until the onions turn translucent, about 3 or 4 minutes.

Transfer the onion-spice mixture to the heated insert of the slow cooker. Add the prepared eggplants, any spices that have fallen onto the plate, the yogurt, the saffron and milk, and the remaining teaspoon of salt. Reduce heat to low. Cover and cook on low heat for 3½ hours; if possible, turn the eggplants over once, to allow the drops of water collected from the steam to fall back into the pan.

Remove the cardamom, cassia pieces, cloves, and bay leaves. Garnish with the cilantro and serve.

:::::::: **NOTE** Indian eggplants are small in size and are often referred to as baby eggplants, though they are fully mature. They can be bought at many specialty markets and at Indian grocers, too. Substitute 6 small Italian eggplants, or small, fat Japanese eggplants if unable to get the Indian variety.

SWEET-AND-SOUR EGGPLANT
khatta meetha baingan

4 tablespoons canola oil, plus 1 tablespoon (optional)

2 pounds small eggplants

2 tablespoons ground coriander

1½ tablespoons roasted ground cumin (see page 12)

1 to 1½ teaspoons ground Indian red chile*

½ teaspoon turmeric

1½ teaspoons green mango powder*

1½ teaspoons salt

2 large ripe tomatoes

2 or 3 serrano chiles, with seeds, sliced lengthwise in thin strips (optional)

Chopped cilantro, for garnish

I have been making this dish since the Bombay Café days. It is probably my most favorite way to eat eggplant, and I tend to include it in many of the cooking classes I teach. Use the small Indian eggplants that are now widely available in specialty stores, at farmers' markets, and of course at the Indian grocer. You can substitute small Japanese eggplants. Adding extra heat to this recipe with fried sliced serrano chiles is, of course, optional!

As eggplants require slow cooking to develop the luscious meaty quality of the vegetable, this recipe translates well to the slow cooker. If you can, do turn them halfway through the cooking process; if that is not convenient, just increase the quantity of tomatoes to 3 large ripe tomatoes to submerge more of the eggplant in the seasonings.

.... SERVES 6 TO 8 ....

Heat the slow cooker on high for 15 minutes; when the insert is warmed through, add 4 tablespoons of the oil and allow to heat while you are stuffing the eggplants.

Trim off the tough ends of the eggplant stems, leaving the caps intact. Make a crosswise slit halfway through each eggplant from the blossom end. Soak them in water to cover for at least ½ hour to open the slits and remove any bitterness.

Mix the spices with ½ teaspoon of the salt in a small bowl. Drain the eggplants in a colander. Working over the bowl containing the spice mix, pry open the slits with your fingers and press a scant ½ teaspoon of the spice mixture into each eggplant, letting any excess fall into the spice bowl. Push the slits to close and to distribute the spices evenly.

Place the spice-filled eggplants, preferably in a single layer, in the heated oil in the slow cooker insert. Sprinkle over the remaining 1 teaspoon of salt and any leftover spice mix. Turn the eggplants once to coat them with the oil. Cover the slow cooker and keep the setting at high while prepping the tomatoes.

Cut the tomatoes in half and, using your palm as a pressure tool, rub the cut side of the halves against the coarse blades of a grater set over a bowl, until only the skin remains. Be careful not to scrape your palms. Discard the skin and pour the tomato pulp over the eggplants. Turn once again to coat the eggplants. Set the slow cooker on low and cook, covered, for 3 hours.

To add more spice to the eggplants, heat the remaining tablespoon of oil in a small skillet and sauté the serrano chiles until lightly blistered. Add to the cooked eggplants. Garnish with the chopped cilantro and serve hot.

CURRIED PEAS AND INDIAN CHEESE
mattar paneer

¼ cup plus 1 tablespoon canola oil

2 medium onions, finely chopped

2 or 3 serrano chiles, coarsely chopped

1 (3-inch) piece fresh ginger, peeled and coarsely chopped

8 or 9 cloves garlic, coarsely chopped

3 medium tomatoes

3 or 4 whole green cardamom pods

3 tablespoons ground coriander

2 tablespoons roasted ground cumin (see page 12)

1 teaspoon ground Indian red chile*

⅓ teaspoon turmeric

1½ teaspoons salt

3 to 3½ cups whey (page 31)

10 ounces frozen peas, defrosted

12 ounces paneer (page 31), cut into cubes

Chopped cilantro, for garnish

There is a saying that if you are at a Punjabi restaurant and ask what vegetarian dishes they have, the answer is as follows: *mattar paneer, paneer mattar*, cheese and peas and peas and cheese! However that may be, this famous vegetable curry is a delicious treat with *chapattis* (page 25) or basmati rice (page 24), and can be served directly from the cooker at large gatherings.

Like most curries, this dish requires some browning of the onions before cooking in the slow cooker. Though I sometimes prepare it by just pureeing the aromatics and combining them with the spices, I prefer to sauté the onions before blending them. I leave it to you to try it both ways and see if you can tell the difference.

SERVES 6 TO 8

Before prepping the ingredients, turn the slow cooker on to the high setting for 15 minutes, until the insert is warmed through. Heat the ¼ cup of oil in a skillet on high heat. Add the onions, lower the heat to medium, and sauté until they turn a deep brown, about 10 to 12 minutes. Cool for 5 minutes.

Put the browned onion mixture, along with the chiles, ginger, and garlic, in a blender and puree. Add the tomatoes and blend thoroughly. Transfer the blended aromatics to the heated insert along with the cardamom, coriander, cumin, chile, turmeric, salt, and whey. Mix well and cook on low for 3 hours.

Add the peas to the curry and continue to cook on low. In a nonstick skillet, heat the remaining tablespoon of oil. Fry half the paneer cubes, turning on all sides to sear evenly; add to the curry. Repeat with the remaining paneer. Continue to cook on low for another 30 minutes. Garnish with cilantro and serve.

SPICY CABBAGE AND PEAS
patta gobi mattar

1 head cabbage
(about 1½ pounds)

1 teaspoon sugar

1 large tomato

2 tablespoons canola oil

1 teaspoon mustard seeds

1 teaspoon cumin seeds

1 (1-inch piece) fresh ginger,
peeled and minced

1 or 2 serrano chiles, coarsely
chopped

1 tablespoon ground coriander

½ teaspoon turmeric

¾ to 1½ teaspoons ground
Indian red chile*

1½ teaspoons salt

8 ounces frozen peas, defrosted

Chopped cilantro, for garnish

I fell in love with the food of the state of Gujarat from the first time I ate it at my college best friend's house. I was invited to lunch by Minal, and I remember this particular dish of cabbage and peas being served that day. Gujaratis love their food hot and spicy, but you can easily adjust the amount of fresh chiles and ground Indian red chile to suit your palate.

One of the key steps to cooking vegetables in India is to soak them in salted water to remove any bitterness. In this recipe, instead of using salt, I soak the cabbage with a spoon of sugar dissolved in the water, thus bringing a little sweetness to the dish.

This recipe requires a 6-quart slow cooker, as the cabbage takes up a good amount of space.

.... SERVES 6 TO 8 ....

Before prepping the ingredients, turn the slow cooker on to the high setting for 15 minutes, until the insert is warmed through.

Cut the cabbage in quarters. Remove the tough core and slice the quarters into ¼-inch strips. Place in a large mixing bowl along with the sugar and enough cool water to cover. Place a plate on top of the cabbage to ensure that it is properly submerged in the water. Set aside.

Cut the tomato in half and, using your palm as a pressure tool, rub the cut side of the halves against the coarse blades of a grater set over a bowl, until only the skin remains. Discard the skin. Be careful not to scrape your palms.

Heat the oil in a small skillet on high heat, with a lid handy. Tilt the pan to pool the oil and carefully add the mustard seeds and cumin seeds; cover immediately to prevent splattering. Remove from the heat and set aside.

Drain the water from the cabbage and put it back in the mixing bowl. Add the grated tomato pulp, ginger, serrano chiles, coriander, turmeric, ground red chile, salt, and the cooked seeds with their oil (use a spoonful of cabbage to get all the oil and seeds from the skillet). Mix thoroughly. Transfer the spiced cabbage to the slow cooker insert and cover. Cook on high for 1 hour. Reduce the cooking temperature to low and continue to cook for 1½ hours.

When the timer goes off, add the peas and continue to cook on low for another 30 minutes. Garnish with chopped cilantro and serve hot.

:::::::: **NOTE** The slow cooker holds the vegetables on warm, but it is best to serve this within an hour. Transfer the cabbage and peas to another dish if you are not serving within an hour. You can reheat this cabbage in a saucepan or skillet on the stovetop on high heat, as there will be enough moisture in the dish.

PUREED SPINACH WITH INDIAN CHEESE
palak paneer

1 (2-inch) piece fresh ginger, peeled and coarsely chopped

5 to 6 cloves garlic, coarsely chopped

2 medium tomatoes, quartered

2 pounds frozen chopped spinach, defrosted

4 tablespoons canola oil

4 small yellow onions, diced small

2 tablespoons chickpea flour*

2 or 3 (½-inch) pieces cassia

6 to 8 cloves

6 to 8 whole black peppercorns

2 or 3 whole black cardamom pods

2 whole bay leaves

3 tablespoons ground coriander

2 teaspoons roasted ground cumin (see page 12)

1 to 1½ teaspoons ground Indian red chile*

½ teaspoon turmeric

½ cup plain yogurt, store-bought or homemade (page 26)

½ cup dried fenugreek leaves*

2 or 3 serrano chiles, halved lengthwise

1½ teaspoons salt

12 ounces paneer, store-bought or homemade (page 31), cut into 1-inch cubes and sautéed (page 31)

Almost every Indian cookbook refers to this dish as *saag paneer,* or mixed greens and cheese. *Palak* is the Indian word for spinach, and as I do not add other greens to my recipe I call it *palak paneer.* There are many variations of this dish; I puree my spinach to attain a velvety texture. This combination of spinach and spices stewing together for a length of time is perfect for the slow cooker.

SERVES 6 TO 8

Before prepping the ingredients, turn the slow cooker on to the high setting for 15 minutes, until the insert is warmed through.

Puree the ginger, garlic, and tomatoes in a blender with a little water and transfer to the slow cooker. In the same blender jar, puree the thawed spinach, using a little water to assist, and add to the cooker. Rinse the jar with a couple of tablespoons of water to get all the pureed spinach out; add this to the cooker.

Heat 3 tablespoons of the oil over high heat in a skillet and add the onions. Turn the heat down to medium-high, stir frequently, and sauté the onions until they are a deep golden brown, about 10 to 12 minutes. Mix in the chickpea flour, stirring to brown and to remove the raw taste. Use a little water to make a paste. Add the mixture to the cooker, then use a little more water to deglaze the hot pan and get out all the granules of the chickpea roux. Add the cassia, cloves, peppercorns, cardamom, bay leaves, coriander, cumin, ground red chile, turmeric, yogurt, fenugreek, serrano chiles, and salt. Mix well and cook on low for 8 hours.

Heat the remaining 1 tablespoon of oil in a nonstick skillet and fry half the paneer cubes, turning on all sides to sear evenly. Remove with a slotted spoon and add to the curry. Repeat with the remaining paneer. Cook for another 15 minutes. Remove the cardamom, cassia pieces, cloves, and bay leaves, and serve.

:::::::: **NOTE** The *palak* can be made ahead of time; when ready to use, bring it to heat and add the seared *paneer* when warmed through.

POTATOES AND PEAS IN TOMATO SAUCE
aloo mattar rasedar

1½ pounds red potatoes

2 tablespoons canola oil

Pinch of asafetida*

1 teaspoon cumin seeds

1 (1-inch) piece fresh ginger, peeled and minced

1 or 2 serrano chiles, minced

2 teaspoons ground coriander

¼ teaspoon turmeric

½ to ¾ teaspoon ground Indian red chile*

1½ teaspoons salt

1 large tomato, quartered

2 whole peeled canned tomatoes

¼ cup water; plus 1 cup hot water

8 ounces frozen green peas

Chopped cilantro for garnish

The combination of potatoes and peas is evident in all regions of India. This version is based on a Gujarati recipe. Light and spicy, it is delicious with hot *chapattis* (page 25) or as a curry on basmati rice (page 24). Serve it with Pork Vindaloo (page 70), or Sautéed Chicken with Green Mango Powder (page 40) for a complete meal. As in many of my recipes, I combine fresh and canned peeled tomatoes here: I get tang from the fresh and substance from the canned. *Aloo mattar rasedar* is probably one of the easier Indian recipes to prepare for the slow cooker. I used a 6-quart cooker for this recipe, however it can be halved and prepared in a 3½-quart slow cooker.

·· SERVES 6 TO 8 ··

Before prepping the ingredients, turn the slow cooker on to the high setting for 15 minutes, until the insert is warmed through. Peel the potatoes, dice into 1½-inch cubes, and soak in water to cover while prepping the rest of the ingredients.

Heat the oil in a small skillet on high heat, with a lid handy. Tilt the pan to pool the oil, add the asafetida, and then carefully add the cumin seeds; cover immediately to prevent splattering. When the seeds finish sputtering, transfer them with their oil to the heated insert.

Drain the potatoes and add to the insert with the ginger, serrano chiles, coriander, turmeric, ground red chile, and salt and stir well. Cover and cook on high while preparing the tomatoes.

Puree the fresh and canned tomatoes in a blender. Add to the potatoes in the insert. Use ¼ cup of warm water to wash the pureed tomatoes from the blender jar, and add this to the insert. Add the frozen peas (do not defrost). Add 1 cup of hot water, or a little less depending on the desired thickness of the sauce. Cover and cook on low for 3½ hours, until the potatoes are cooked through. Depending on the age of the potatoes, this may take 30 minutes more or less. It is best to check after 3 hours of cooking to determine how much longer it may take to cook the potatoes through.

Garnish with the cilantro and serve hot.

PUMPKIN WITH FENNEL AND TAMARIND CHUTNEY
kadu ki sabzi

2 tablespoons canola oil

1 teaspoon fennel seeds

2 pounds pumpkin, peeled and cut into 2-inch pieces

1 (½-inch) piece fresh ginger, peeled and julienned

½ teaspoon ginger powder*

½ teaspoon turmeric

1½ teaspoons ground Indian red chile*

1 teaspoon ground roasted cumin (see page 12)

1 teaspoon salt

⅓ cup or more tamarind chutney (see Note)

Chopped cilantro, for garnish

I have to admit that growing up in a boarding school, I was subjected to awful preparations of certain vegetables. Pumpkin was one of them. It was not until I came to the United States and had it in the form of a sweet pie at Thanksgiving, as a soup, and, later, as a filling for ravioli, that I would willingly try a taste of any dish with pumpkins.

When I was researching some of the recipes for this book in India, my sister's husband and in-laws insisted I include this recipe. Gopi, their cook, and I made it in the slow cooker, and we were all delighted at what a wonderful dish it was. Use other winter squashes such as butternut or acorn squash, either in combination or just the one you like. The spices take the vegetable to another level.

SERVES 6 TO 8

Before prepping the ingredients, turn the slow cooker on to the high setting for 15 minutes, until the insert is warmed through.

Heat the oil in a small skillet on high heat. Tilt the pan to pool the oil and carefully add the fennel seeds; sauté for 30 seconds, stirring constantly so they do not burn. Add seeds and oil to the insert of the slow cooker along with the pumpkin, fresh ginger, ginger powder, turmeric, chile, cumin, and salt. Cook for 4 hours on low. Once the squash is cooked, stir in the tamarind chutney; taste and add more chutney if desired. Serve garnished with chopped cilantro.

:::::::: **NOTE** Tamarind chutney is sold at most Indian stores; a recipe is also included on page 48.

dals

On one of my weekly jaunts to the Indian grocery store in Fairfield, California, about a twenty-minute ride from my former restaurant, Neela's, in downtown Napa, I was once again struck by the number of dals available for sale. The shelves were packed with a plethora of legumes, lentils, and beans in a multitude of colors and sizes.

The slow cooker may as well have been invented for lentils, legumes, and beans. Though today many Indians have switched to cooking these in a pressure cooker, the end result from slow cooking is far superior. Many legumes and beans need to stew for several hours, sometimes as long as overnight, and that is where the slow cooker excels. I have included recipes for both dals (simmered legume dishes) and bean preparations in this chapter.

Lentils and beans translate to the slow cooker easily, but to transform them into a finished dish it is imperative to add the *tadka* or tempered spices. When this step is to be done at the time of serving, my suggestion is to cook the lentils earlier in the day and when you're ready to serve, heat through the amount needed for the meal, adding a little hot water if need be to adjust the texture, tasting for salt, and then finishing it with the *tadka*. Cooking the dal earlier in the day or the day before will also free up your slow cooker for preparing a curry or a side vegetable to serve with the dal.

Many lentils and beans are imported and due to strict regulations are without foreign objects such as small stones and sticks. But I still recommend sifting through to ensure that there are none before you wash them in several rinses of water. Soaking is no longer a necessity as the slow cooker eliminates this step.

MERCIN'S LEMON DAL
khatti dal

1½ cups pink lentils*

4½ to 5 cups hot water

1 small yellow onion,
diced small

4 cloves garlic,
sliced in thin rounds

1 (½-inch) piece fresh ginger,
peeled and minced

2 or 3 serrano chiles,
sliced in thin rounds

1½ teaspoons salt

2 tablespoons lemon juice

1 tablespoon milk

TADKA

1½ tablespoons ghee

1 heaping teaspoon brown
mustard seeds

6 or 7 fresh kari leaves*

This is one of my favorite dals; I put it in my first cookbook, *The Bombay Café*, so needless to say I had to cook it in the slow cooker just so that I could include it in this book, too. Mercin was my nanny, and she brought this recipe to our dinner table. My husband eats it like soup; I like to pour it over plain basmati rice (page 24); and my children and grandchildren relate to it as comfort food.

This recipe does not take long in the slow cooker. I cook it on high, but if you wished to set it to cook and run errands you could use the low setting and extend the time to five hours. Adjust the amount of water depending on what consistency you want.

SERVES 6 TO 8

Before prepping the ingredients, turn the slow cooker on to the high setting for 15 minutes, until the insert is warmed through.

Pick over the lentils for any foreign objects. Wash the lentils in a bowl in several changes of water until the last wash runs almost clear. Place the lentils along with the water, onion, garlic, ginger, chiles, and salt in the cooker. Stir well and set to cook on high for 2½ hours. When the lentils are cooked, they will be pale yellow in color. Add the lemon juice, stir, and adjust the seasoning, adding more lemon juice if preferred. Add the milk and stir.

To make the *tadka*, heat the ghee in a small saucepan or skillet, with a lid handy. Tilt the pan to form a pool, add the mustard seeds and kari leaves, and cover immediately. Once the seeds have finished sputtering, add the *tadka* to the lentils, stir, and serve hot.

BROWN LENTILS WITH ONIONS, TOMATOES, AND GINGER

sabath masoor ki dal

1½ cups whole brown lentils*

6 cups hot water

1 large yellow onion, diced small

1 (1½-inch) piece fresh ginger, peeled and minced

4 or 5 cloves garlic, minced

2 medium tomatoes, diced small

1 or 2 serrano chiles, chopped

¼ teaspoon turmeric

½ to ¾ teaspoon ground Indian red chile*

1½ teaspoons salt

1 tablespoon ghee

Pinch of asafetida*

1 teaspoon cumin seeds

Chopped cilantro, for garnish

The brown lentils used in India are the whole unhusked red lentils known as *sabath masoor*. This is the easiest dal preparation for the Western kitchen, as these lentils are available in most supermarkets and do not require a special visit to an Indian grocery store. Franklin, my husband, prefers this particular dal, which he compares to a lentil soup. His favorite way to eat it is with basmati rice (page 24) and Cauliflower with Ginger and Cumin (page 80).

Once again the advantage of using the slow cooker for this recipe is that it allows the dal to stew slowly. The seasoning mix or *tadka* is added at the beginning, making the dal ready to ladle out when done without further ado.

·· SERVES 6 TO 8 ··

Before prepping the ingredients, turn the slow cooker on to the high setting for 15 minutes, until the insert is warmed through.

Pick over the lentils for any foreign objects. Wash the lentils in a bowl in several changes of water until the last wash runs almost clear. Add the lentils, water, onions, ginger, garlic, tomatoes, serrano chiles, turmeric, ground red chile, and salt.

Heat the ghee in a small saucepan or skillet and carefully add the asafetida and the cumin seeds. When they finish sputtering, about a minute, add to the lentils in the slow cooker. Cook on low for 8 hours. Serve garnished with cilantro.

YELLOW MUNG BEANS WITH FRESH SPINACH
moong aur palak ki dal

1⅓ cups yellow mung beans*

4½ cups hot water

1½ teaspoons salt

3 cups fresh spinach leaves, stems removed, washed several times

TADKA

2 tablespoons ghee

Pinch of asafetida*

1 teaspoon cumin seeds

1 tablespoon crushed red pepper flakes

2 teaspoons minced garlic

2 teaspoons minced peeled ginger

Chandan used to cook some of the specialties from his home region in the mountains just south of the Himalayas, including this particular dal. It takes its flavor from the addition of fresh spinach leaves and the roasting of garlic and ginger in the ghee; the heat comes from the crushed red chiles. Although this dish is great by itself, serving it with Lamb Chops with Browned Onions and Tomatoes (page 73) or Roast Chicken à la Rama (page 60), along with either rice or flat bread, makes for a scrumptious meal.

The spinach needs to be added after the beans are cooked and while the cooker is still on the warm mode. This prevents the leaves from totally disintegrating into the dal.

······································· SERVES 6 TO 8 ·······································

Before prepping the ingredients, turn the slow cooker on to the high setting for 15 minutes, until the insert is warmed through.

Pick over the mung beans for any foreign objects. Wash them in a bowl in several changes of water till the last wash runs almost clear. Add the mung beans to the slow cooker along with the water and salt and cook for 3½ hours on low.

When the timer sounds and the cooker is on the warm setting, add the spinach leaves and mix well. Allow the leaves to wilt into the hot mung beans. If not serving within 30 minutes, turn the machine off and remove the insert.

When ready to serve, reheat the mung beans if necessary and put them in a serving dish. Heat the ghee in a small skillet on high heat. Carefully add the asafetida and the cumin seeds and, when they stop sputtering, add the garlic and ginger and cook for 1 or 2 minutes, stirring frequently to prevent burning. As the garlic starts to turn color, add the red pepper flakes and pour the tadka on top of the prepared lentils.

MIXED YELLOW DAL
bengali dal

⅔ cup yellow mung beans*

⅔ cup pigeon peas*

⅔ cup pink lentils*

1 (1-inch) piece fresh ginger, peeled and minced

3 large cloves garlic, minced

1½ teaspoons salt

5½ cups hot water

Juice of two lemons, about 2 tablespoons

TADKA

3 tablespoons ghee

Large pinch of asafetida*

1 teaspoon brown mustard seeds

2 teaspoons cumin seeds

1 teaspoon nigella seeds*

2 or 3 serrano chiles, cut lengthwise into 6 pieces

4 whole dried red árbol chiles

8 to 10 kari leaves*

Chopped cilantro, for garnish

On one of my visits with a cousin in New Jersey, I got to relish a most delicious yet simple dal, made by my cousin's wife, who is from Bengal. Later, when they were visiting me in California, it happened to be the dal of the day at Neela's, my restaurant in Napa. Though not an exact interpretation, she loved it!

Serve it with basmati rice (page 24), Pureed Spinach with Indian Cheese (page 92) and Braised Chicken with Dried Fenugreek (page 57). This recipe serves 6 to 8 and can easily be cut in half and cooked in a smaller, 3½-quart slow cooker. The *tadka* amounts are also measured for the full recipe, so halve those, too.

·· SERVES 6 TO 8 ··

Before prepping the ingredients, turn the slow cooker on to the high setting for 15 minutes, until the insert is warmed through.

Pick over all the mung beans and lentils for any foreign objects. Wash them in a bowl in several changes of water until the last wash runs almost clear. Put the mung beans, lentils, ginger, garlic, salt, and water in the insert of the slow cooker and set it to cook on high for 3 hours. After 3 hours, carefully remove the cover and continue to cook on high for another 15 minutes to reduce extra liquid. Stir in the lemon juice.

Prepare the *tadka* by heating the ghee in a small skillet, with a lid handy. Tilt the skillet to one side and quickly add the asafetida, mustard seeds, cumin seeds, nigella seeds, chiles, and kari leaves, covering immediately to prevent splattering. When the sizzling subsides, pour the *tadka* over the hot lentils. Serve garnished with chopped cilantro.

GREEN MUNG BEANS WITH BROWNED ONIONS
hari moong dal

1¼ cups whole green mung beans*

6 cups hot water

3 cloves garlic, thinly sliced lengthwise

1 (½-inch) piece fresh ginger, peeled and cut in thin julienne

¼ teaspoon turmeric

1¼ teaspoons salt

2 small tomatoes, cut into 6 wedges each

TADKA

3 tablespoons ghee

Pinch of asafetida*

1½ teaspoons cumin seeds

1 medium yellow onion, thinly sliced

1 teaspoon crushed red pepper flakes

Whole green mung beans are available in almost all grocery stores throughout the United States. They make a hearty dal that is best served with *chapattis* (page 25) and a vegetable dish such as Spicy Cabbage and Peas (page 90). The browned onion *tadka*, added right before serving, perks up the flavor of the beans.

·· SERVES 6 TO 8 ··

Before prepping the ingredients, turn the slow cooker on to the high setting for 15 minutes, until the insert is warmed through.

Pick over the mung beans for any foreign objects. Wash the beans in a bowl in several changes of water until the last wash runs almost clear. Place the beans along with the hot water, garlic, ginger, turmeric, and salt in the slow cooker insert. Turn the cooker to low and cook for 5 hours.

When the beans are done cooking, add the tomatoes and maintain the cooker on warm for no more than half an hour (this is done to keep the tomatoes from totally falling apart). After that, it is best to use the dal or cool it and store for later usage.

Over high heat, heat the ghee in a small saucepan with a lid handy. Tilt the pan to pool the ghee and add the asafetida and cumin seeds; cover to contain the sputtering. When the sizzling dies down, add the onions and fry on high for 4 to 5 minutes, stirring constantly to avoid burning. Once the onions are deep brown in color, add the red pepper, mix well, immediately pour over the hot beans, and serve.

PINK LENTILS WITH TOMATOES AND KARI LEAVES
masoor tamatar dal

1½ cups pink lentils*

4½ cups hot water

1 small yellow onion, diced small

4 cloves garlic, sliced in thin rounds

2 small tomatoes, diced

2 or 3 serrano chiles, sliced in thin rounds

1½ teaspoons salt

TADKA

1½ tablespoons ghee

1 teaspoon cumin seeds

6 or 7 kari leaves*

There are so many varieties of dal, but whenever Franklin and I discuss what to eat for dinner, I lean toward this recipe. We find it light, flavorful, spicy, and easy to pair with just about any vegetable or nonvegetarian curry, such as Ground Meat with Potatoes and Peas (page 77). If you prefer to lessen the heat, just reduce the quantity of the serrano chiles.

This dal is usually cooked to the point where the lentils still have a little shape to them; this means that the aromatics can cook along with the lentils in the slow cooker and they remain somewhat firm. The dal is then seasoned with a *tadka* of the spices just before serving.

SERVES 6 TO 8

Before prepping the ingredients, turn the slow cooker on to the high setting for 15 minutes, until the insert is warmed through. Pick over the lentils for any foreign objects. Wash the lentils in a bowl in several changes of water until the last wash runs almost clear. Place the lentils along with the water, onion, garlic, tomatoes, chiles, and salt in the cooker. Stir well and set to cook on high for 3 hours.

When ready to serve, prepare the *tadka*. Heat the ghee in a small saucepan or skillet, with a cover handy. Tilt the pan to form a pool and add the cumin seeds and kari leaves; cover immediately to prevent splattering. Once they have finished sizzling, add to the lentils, stir, and serve hot.

WHOLE BLACK LENTILS
makhni dal

2 cups black lentils*

6 cups hot water

⅓ cup tomato sauce

¼ cup heavy cream

2 or 3 cloves garlic, minced

1 (1½-inch) piece fresh ginger, peeled and minced

1 teaspoon ground Indian red chile*

1½ teaspoons salt

TADKA

2 tablespoons ghee

3 or 4 whole dried red árbol chiles, broken in two

1 teaspoon cumin seeds, for garnish (optional)

Butter, for garnish

Small black lentils are a must in North Indian restaurants and a given in most Punjabi homes. The creaminess of these legumes and the addition of cream and butter give this dish the name *makhni dal*, or buttery lentils.

Made traditionally, these lentils require soaking overnight and cooking on a low heat for hours with constant tending, as they do burn at the bottom of the saucepan once the lentils break open. The advantage of the slow cooker is that one does not need to either soak them or tend to them during the cooking process. I find cooking this dal overnight a big help, as I can then free up the slow cooker to make another dish.

·· SERVES 8 ··

Before prepping the ingredients, turn the slow cooker on to the high setting for 15 minutes, until the insert is warmed through.

Pick over the lentils for any foreign objects. Wash the lentils in a bowl in several changes of water until the last wash runs almost clear. Place the lentils, water, tomato sauce, cream, garlic, ginger, chile, and salt in the slow cooker insert and stir to mix well. Cook on low for 10 hours, until the lentils are cooked through and the dal has a creamy texture. If you're not using them right away, cool the lentils and store them in the refrigerator, reheating thoroughly when it's time to add the *tadka* and serve.

Prepare the *tadka* by heating the ghee in a small skillet on high heat, with a lid handy. Tilt the pan to pool the ghee and add the árbol chiles and cumin seeds, covering to contain the splattering. After they sizzle for a minute, pour the *tadka* over the hot dal, top with a pat of butter if desired, and serve.

CHICKPEAS WITH VEGETABLES
pahari dal

2 cups small chickpeas
(channa dal)*

5½ cups hot water

¼ teaspoon turmeric

1 teaspoon ground
Indian red chile*

1½ teaspoons salt

TADKA

2 tablespoons ghee

Pinch of asafetida*

1 teaspoon cumin seeds

1 small yellow onion,
diced small

3 cloves garlic, minced

1 (1½-inch) piece fresh ginger,
peeled and minced

2 serrano chiles, halved
lengthwise and cut into
half moons

2 small tomatoes, diced

1 tablespoon ground coriander

1 teaspoon green
mango powder*

¼ cup warm water

2 medium Yukon gold potatoes,
peeled and cut into 1-inch cubes

1 small daikon, peeled and cut
into ¼-inch half disks, with
diced tender leaves stems if
available

½ small cauliflower, cut into
small florets, with sliced tender
leaves if available

Chopped cilantro, for garnish

During a holiday that I took with my parents to the Kullu Valley in northeastern India, we came across a military encampment at lunch. It was there that I learned how to prepare this hearty dal. Serve it with either plain basmati rice (page 25) or *chapattis* (page 24). If possible, do add the leaves of both the daikon and the cauliflower, which lend an additional layer of flavor to the dish. Alternatively, you can add 2 cups of fresh spinach leaves at the end of cooking so the residual heat just wilts the leaves. Adjust the heat level by adding more or less of the green chiles and ground red chile.

Though these chickpeas are perfect for cooking in a slow cooker, this recipe does require some additional attention, as the vegetables have to be added in stages lest they become water-laden from stewing too long.

··· SERVES 6 TO 8 ···

Before prepping the ingredients, turn the slow cooker on to the high setting for 15 minutes, until the insert is warmed through.

Pick over the chickpeas for any foreign objects. Wash them in a bowl in several changes of water until the last wash runs almost clear. Place the chickpeas and the hot water in the insert of the slow cooker. Add the turmeric, ½ teaspoon of the ground red chile, and 1 teaspoon of the salt. Cook on high, covered, while preparing the *tadka*.

Heat the ghee in a large skillet on high. Add the asafetida and the cumin seeds, and, as soon as the seeds sizzle, add the onions, garlic, and ginger. Fry on high heat until the onions turn brown at the edges, 8 to 10 minutes. Add the serrano chiles and tomatoes, then the ground coriander and mango powder and continue to fry, smashing the tomatoes lightly with the back of the spoon. Add the remaining teaspoon of the salt and ½ teaspoon ground red chile. Add this *tadka* to the dal in the slow cooker. Pour ¼ cup of warm water into the skillet used for the *tadka*, scrape and stir to deglaze the remaining *tadka*, and add this to the lentils. Turn the slow cooker to low and cook for 4 hours.

After 4 hours, add the potatoes and continue to cook for 1 hour, then add the daikon and its leaves. After another hour, add the cauliflower and its leaves and cook for 1 more hour. Garnish with chopped cilantro and serve hot.

CURRIED CHICKPEAS
channa masala

2 cups chickpeas

5 to 6½ cups hot water, depending on desired consistency

2 black cardamom pods

2 (1-inch) pieces cassia

4 to 6 cloves

2 bay leaves

¼ teaspoon turmeric

¼ teaspoon ground Indian red chile*

1½ to 2 teaspoons salt

MASALA

3 tablespoons canola oil

1 large yellow onion, diced small

6 cloves garlic, coarsely chopped

1 (2-inch) piece fresh ginger, peeled and coarsely chopped

1 medium tomato, coarsely chopped

2 whole peeled canned tomatoes

1½ tablespoons ground coriander

2 teaspoons roasted ground cumin (see page 12)

¼ teaspoon turmeric

¼ teaspoon ground Indian red chile*

¾ teaspoon green mango powder*

½ teaspoon black salt*

½ teaspoon ground black pepper

2 serrano chiles, halved lengthwise

¼ cup water

Chopped cilantro, for garnish

Many times during my college days, I'd come home in the late afternoon and raid the kitchen, hoping that Chandan, our cook, had prepared *channa masala* that day. His preparation had a lot of gravy and chiles, and was delightful over rice in a bowl along with some *kachumber*, Chopped Salad of Tomatoes, Cucumbers, and Red Onions (page 108). I simply loved it! The recipe here is more in keeping with the traditional amount of masala or gravy, but should you wish to thin it out, just add more water (I have given you a range). You may also adjust the salt, and maybe add some more chile!

Sometimes I think that the slow cooker was built specifically for dishes like this one. In the past, one would have to remember to soak the chickpeas overnight to soften, and then cook them for hours. With the slow cooker, one can rest assured that after 10 hours of stewing without attention, the chickpeas are cooked to perfection.

SERVES 6 TO 8

Pick over the beans for foreign objects. Add the chickpeas, water, cardamom, cassia, cloves, bay leaves, turmeric, ground red chile, and salt to the cooker. Cover and cook on high while preparing the masala.

Heat the oil in a large frying pan on medium-high heat. Add the onions and fry until golden brown, about 10 to 12 minutes. While the onions are browning, puree the garlic and ginger with a little water in a blender until smooth. Transfer to a small bowl. Puree the tomatoes in the same blender jar without rinsing. Once the onions are golden brown, add the garlic-ginger puree and the coriander, cumin, turmeric, ground red chile, mango powder, black salt, and black pepper and fry with the onions for 2 or 3 minutes. Add the pureed tomatoes and cook for 2 or 3 more minutes to incorporate all the spices. Add the serrano chiles, and then add this masala to the slow cooker. Pour ¼ cup of water into the pan to deglaze, and add that also. Cover and cook for 10 hours on low.

Remove the cardamom, cassia pieces, cloves, and bay leaves, garnish with chopped cilantro, and serve hot.

:::::::: **NOTE** You can substitute 1½ cups of Basic Curry Mix (page 54) for the masala, adding the mango powder, black salt, black pepper, and serrano chiles. Heat it thoroughly before using.

BLACK-EYED PEA CURRY
rasedar lobia

2 cups dried black-eyed peas*

5 cups hot water

1½ teaspoons salt

3 tablespoons canola oil

½ teaspoon cumin seeds

1 medium yellow onion, minced

4 or 5 cloves garlic, coarsely chopped

1 (1½-inch) piece fresh ginger, peeled and coarsely chopped

2 large tomatoes, diced small

1½ tablespoons ground coriander

1 teaspoon roasted ground cumin (see page 12)

1 teaspoon or less ground Indian red chile*

½ teaspoon turmeric

Chopped cilantro, for garnish

All over India, beans are used as an important source of protein. Black-eyed peas are known as *lobia* or *raungi*. Chandan made this curry with a lot of gravy, giving it a soup like consistency. We ate it with rice or *chapattis*, but it can easily be served as a soup. Adding sautéed Portuguese or Moroccan sausages gives it a completely non-Indian but delicious twist, as does serving it with crostini .

·· SERVES 8 ··

Pick over the peas for foreign objects. Add the peas, water, and salt to the slow cooker, cover, and cook on high.

In a saucepan or large skillet, heat the oil on high. Add the cumin seeds and when they finish sputtering, turn the heat to medium-high and add the onions. Stir frequently for about 10 to 12 minutes to get an even browning.

Puree the garlic and ginger in a blender with a little bit of water; add this to the browned onions and mix well. Add the tomatoes along with the coriander, cumin, ground red chile, and turmeric and fry on high heat, smashing the tomatoes down with the back of the spoon to bind the aromatics and spices together. Add this prepared masala to the chickpeas in the slow cooker, reduce the heat to low, and cook for 6 hours. Garnish with cilantro and serve.

RED KIDNEY BEANS
rajma

2 cups dried red kidney beans

1 medium yellow onion, coarsely chopped

1 (1½-inch) piece fresh ginger, peeled or coarsely chopped

3 cloves garlic, coarsely chopped

2 medium tomatoes, quartered

6 cups water

1 or 2 serrano chiles, chopped

1 tablespoon ground coriander

1 teaspoon roasted ground cumin (see page 12)

¼ teaspoon turmeric

½ to 1 teaspoon ground Indian red chile*

1½ teaspoons salt

¼ cup chopped cilantro, for garnish

Beans are cooked as a main dish all over India, as many Indians are vegetarian. The serving of *rajma* and basmati rice (page 24) is a common meal in most homes, especially for lunch, often accompanied by a raita (page 28) and *kachumber* (page 27).

Traditionally, one would first stew the beans until halfway cooked, then add the aromatics and spices sautéed in ghee or oil and continue to stew until the beans are fork tender. I have found that with a slow cooker, you can incorporate the seasonings from the beginning, making for a butter- or oil-free recipe that still keeps the integrity of the original dish.

SERVES 6 TO 8

Before prepping the ingredients, turn the slow cooker on to the high setting for 15 minutes, until the insert is warmed through.

Pick through the beans for any stones or debris and wash them in a bowl in several changes of water, until the last wash runs almost clear.

Mince the onions, ginger, garlic, and tomatoes into a fine paste in a food processor. Add this mix along with the water, serrano chiles, coriander, cumin, turmeric, ground red chile, and salt to the slow cooker and cook on low for 8 hours. Garnish with cilantro and serve hot.

rice dishes

For the first several years of my life in the United States, I cooked and ate rice with all my Indian meals. I did not yet know how to prepare *chapattis*, and was actually afraid of the task. After all, back home I was used to sitting at the dining table and being served puffed, light, delicious flat bread one by one until I was satisfied.

But it was no hardship for me to rely on rice. I come from the land of basmati, termed the queen of rice for its long, individual grains and its aromatic and nutty character. So first I learned to perfect plain *chawal* (page 24) and then ventured into adding flavors through spices and vegetables. I was determined to make rice shine. With time, I was able to present *pullaos* and *biryanis* at the dinner table with confidence.

When it came to making rice in a slow cooker, I wanted to make it perfect, each grain separate and each flavor distinct. I was not sure this could be done so I began researching techniques, and modifying and testing my tried and true recipes. To my amazement, it all worked very well indeed; simply follow the directions in the recipes.

In this chapter, I offer you not just *pullaos* (rice cooked with vegetables) and *biryanis* (rice layered with spiced meats or poultry and cooked in sealed vessels), but also *khichdi*, which combine rice and lentils and can range from a soupy rendition to one where the grains and lentils stand up for themselves. The slow cooker is perfect for these, as they need to be on the mushy side.

rice preparation 101

Today many brands of basmati rice are well processed, giving us almost no foreign objects in the rice. But just to be sure, pick through the rice and then wash it—a step that helps remove the talc that the rice has been treated with for preservation. To wash, gently swish the measured amount of rice in a mixing bowl of water, using light movements of the hand, as the delicate grains can easily break. I use a mixing bowl with a lip, as it allows me to drain the water without losing too many of the rice grains. Rinse and drain the rice at least four or five times in cool water, and when ready to cook, soak it in the measured amount of tepid water as specified in each recipe. Soaking helps elongate the basmati rice grains.

When the timer for the rice goes off, turn the power off and remove the insert unless otherwise directed in the recipe. Cover with a piece of paper towel to absorb the steam in the insert, place the lid back on the insert, and wait 2 to 3 minutes before uncovering and fluffing the rice with a fork. At this point replace the lid slightly askew, leaving a small gap open. This helps keep the rice from becoming mushy and sticky.

BASMATI RICE WITH BROWNED ONIONS
bhuga chawal

1½ cups basmati rice

2 tablespoons ghee

2 whole black cardamom pods

2 (1½-inch) pieces cassia

4 or 5 whole cloves

1 small yellow onion, sliced thin

1½ teaspoons salt

2¾ cups hot water

In the cuisine of Sindh, my mother's province in northwestern India, *bhuga chawal* is one of the more aromatic ways of preparing rice. It is imperative to get the onions dark brown in color without burning them to impart both flavor and color to the dish. Once the onions have been browned, this recipe can be finished in the slow cooker. Preparing flavored rice in the slow cooker has the advantage of holding it warm until ready to eat; however, do be careful to turn the machine off after half an hour or less on the warm setting, as it will dry the bottom layer of the rice. The recipe can be doubled or tripled in the same size cooker.

.... SERVES 6 ....

Before prepping the ingredients, turn the slow cooker on to the high setting for 15 minutes, until the insert is warmed through.

Pick over the rice, removing any foreign objects. In a bowl, wash the rice gently in several changes of cold water until the water runs clear. Soak the rice in warm water while preparing the seasonings.

Heat 1½ tablespoons of the ghee in a skillet over high heat. Add the cardamom, cassia, and cloves and fry for a few seconds before adding the onions. Fry until they start to turn light brown, stirring constantly; reduce the heat to medium and continue to sauté until dark brown, 8 to 10 minutes. Be careful not to burn the onions.

Brush the remaining ghee on the bottom and an inch up the sides of the cooking insert (alternatively you can spray it with butter-flavored cooking spray). Drain the rice and transfer it to the cooking insert along with the salt, hot water, and onion-spice mix. Cover and cook on high for 1½ hours. Halfway through the cooking process, stir the rice to bring the water up from the bottom.

When the timer sounds and the cooker reverts to the automatic warm setting, remove the lid, place a paper towel over the rice to absorb additional moisture, and place the lid back on. Let stand for 15 minutes on the warm setting before uncovering. Remove the paper and fluff the rice with a flat spatula or fork and serve while still steaming hot. I prefer to leave the whole spices in this recipe as they continue to flavor the rice; they are easily visible and can be pushed to the side when eating the dish. However, you can remove them if you like.

SPICED RICE WITH POTATOES AND PEAS
masala chawal

1½ cups basmati rice

3 medium red potatoes, peeled and cut in 1-inch cubes

2 teaspoons ghee

2¾ cups boiling hot water

½ teaspoon brown mustard seeds

1 teaspoon cumin seeds

6 to 8 fresh kari leaves*

2 serrano chiles, finely chopped

1 (1-inch) piece fresh ginger, peeled and minced

2 small tomatoes, diced

¼ teaspoon turmeric

½ teaspoon ground Indian red chile*

1 teaspoon garam masala, store-bought or homemade (page 34, variation)

1¼ teaspoons salt

¼ cup chopped cilantro

⅓ cup grated coconut meat*

8 ounces frozen peas, defrosted

My aunt Vrinda, who taught me the nuances of how to use spices, would often prepare this recipe for dinner. She and I would eat it with either a raita or a chutney, but her English husband would pair it with store-bought roasted chicken he picked up on the way home from work. I suggest you try it with Roast Chicken à la Rama (page 60), raita (page 28), and Sweet Tomato Chutney (page 50).

The rice will cook faster than the potatoes, so I boil these until they are halfway cooked before proceeding. I also add the defrosted peas after the timer has turned to the warm setting, cooking them in the residual heat.

.... SERVES 6 TO 8 ....

Before prepping the ingredients, turn the slow cooker on to the high setting for 15 minutes, until the insert is warmed through.

Pick over the rice to remove any foreign objects. Gently wash the rice in a bowl in several changes of water until the last wash runs almost clear. Boil the potatoes until halfway done, about 4 minutes. They should still be firm in the center when pierced with a knife tip. Drain and set aside.

Brush 1 teaspoon of the ghee on the bottom and an inch up the sides of the heated insert (alternatively you can spray it with butter-flavored cooking spray). Drain the rice and transfer it to the cooker insert along with the potatoes; add the boiling water.

Heat a small skillet on high heat, with a lid handy. Add the remaining 1 teaspoon of ghee, tilt the skillet to form a pool, and carefully add the mustard seeds and, quickly, the cumin seeds. As they sizzle, add the kari leaves, green chiles, and ginger, cover to prevent spattering. Take the skillet off the heat and stir in the tomatoes, turmeric, red chile, and garam masala. Mix and add to the rice, pouring a little water into the skillet to deglaze, and add this to the insert. Add the salt, cilantro, and coconut. Stir to mix, cover, and cook on high for 1½ hours. During the cooking process, stir the rice twice, gently.

When the timer sounds, stir in the defrosted peas, cover, and continue to steam in the cooker on the warm setting for another 10 minutes.

Turn off the slow cooker, remove the lid, and cover the rice with a paper towel. Place the lid back on the cooker, and let stand for another 5 minutes. Remove the lid and paper towel and fluff with a fork. Serve hot. If the rice is to be served later, transfer it to a serving dish, spreading the *pullao* out to ensure that it does not clump up. To reheat, cover the rice with a damp paper towel, seal the dish with aluminum foil, and bake at 350°F for 5 to 6 minutes.

RICE WITH CHICKPEAS
channa pullao

1½ cups basmati rice

2 tablespoons ghee

2¾ cups boiling water, plus
1 tablespoon water

24 ounces canned chickpeas,
rinsed and drained

½ teaspoon brown
mustard seeds

1 teaspoon cumin seeds

6 to 8 fresh kari leaves*

2 serrano chiles, finely chopped

1 (1-inch) piece fresh ginger,
peeled and minced

1 large yellow onion, sliced thin

2 small tomatoes, sliced thin

¼ teaspoon turmeric

½ teaspoon ground
Indian red chile*

1½ teaspoons salt

Wanting to give my husband Franklin some flavors from his native Cuba, I remembered this rice and bean recipe from my earlier days in India. *Channa pullao* is the perfect accompaniment to either Yogurt and Black Pepper Chicken (page 65) or Browned Lamb with Onions, Tomatoes, and Spices (page 75).

························· SERVES 6 TO 8 ·························

Before prepping the ingredients, turn the slow cooker on to the high setting for 15 minutes, until the insert is warmed through.

Pick over the rice for any foreign objects. In a bowl, wash the rice gently in several changes of cold water until the water runs clear. Soak the rice in warm water for 12 to 15 minutes.

Brush 1 teaspoon of the ghee on the bottom and an inch up the sides of the heated insert (alternatively you can spray it with butter-flavored cooking spray). Drain the rice and transfer it along with the chickpeas to the cooker insert; add the boiling water.

Heat the remaining ghee in a large skillet on high, with a lid handy. Tilt the skillet to pool the ghee and carefully add the mustard seeds and then, quickly, the cumin seeds; cover to prevent spattering. As they sizzle, add the kari leaves, green chiles, and ginger and cover again until the spattering eases.

Add the sliced onions and sauté for 2 to 3 minutes until they turn translucent. Add the tomatoes and fry for another minute. Transfer to the insert and pour 1 tablespoon of water into the skillet to deglaze the spices; add this to the insert. Cover and cook on high for 1½ hours. During the cooking process, stir the rice twice, gently.

When the timer sounds, turn off the slow cooker, remove the lid, and cover the rice with a paper towel. Place the lid back on the cooker, and let stand for another 15 minutes. Remove the paper towel and fluff with a fork. Serve hot.

MIXED VEGETABLE RICE
sabzi pullao

1½ cups basmati rice

2 teaspoons ghee

2¾ cups boiling water

½ teaspoon brown mustard seeds

1 teaspoon cumin seeds

6 to 8 fresh kari leaves*

1 (1-inch) piece fresh ginger, peeled and julienned

1¼ teaspoons salt

12 ounces frozen mixed vegetables, defrosted

More often than not, Indians will eat plain steamed rice with their highly seasoned curries, dals, and vegetables, but when it comes time to entertain they either add a simple spice such as cumin seeds or make a highly seasoned *pullao*, rice with vegetables or meat. *Sabzi pullao*, a vegetarian dish, was a mainstay at the Bombay Café. We served it along with Pink Lentils with Tomatoes and Kari Leaves (page 105) and raita (page 28).

Here in the United States, we have the conveniences of vegetables that are diced, cooked, and frozen for instant use. I find using a small bag of mixed vegetables including peas, corn, green beans, and carrots very convenient. However, if you prefer to prep your vegetables for this recipe, cut them all of equal size and cook them in lightly salted water before using as described in the final steps below.

·· SERVES 6 TO 8 ··

Before prepping the ingredients, turn the slow cooker on to the high setting for 15 minutes, until the insert is warmed through.

Pick over the rice, removing any foreign objects. In a bowl, wash the rice gently in several changes of cold water until the water runs clear. Soak the rice in warm water for 12 to 15 minutes. .

Brush 1 teaspoon of the ghee on the bottom and an inch up the sides of the heated cooking insert (alternatively you can spray it with butter-flavored cooking spray). Drain the rice, transfer it to the cooker insert, and add the boiling water.

Heat a small skillet on high heat, with a lid handy. Add the remaining teaspoon of ghee and tilt the skillet to form a pool of the butter. Carefully add the mustard seeds and, quickly, the cumin seeds. As they start to sizzle, add the kari leaves and ginger and cover to avoid spattering. Add this *tadka* to the rice and water with the salt, mix gently, and cook on high for 1½ hours. During the cooking process, stir the rice twice, gently.

When the timer sounds and the cooker switches over to the warm setting, stir in the defrosted vegetables, cover, and continue to steam in the cooker on the warm setting for another 20 minutes.

Turn off the slow cooker, remove the lid, and cover the rice with a paper towel. Place the lid back on the cooker and let stand for another 15 minutes. Remove the lid and paper towel and fluff with a fork. Serve hot. If the rice is to be served later, transfer it to a serving dish and spread it out to ensure that it does not clump up. To reheat, cover the rice with a damp paper towel, seal the dish with aluminum foil, and bake at 350°F for 5 to 6 minutes.

CHICKEN LAYERED WITH RICE
murgh ki biryani

2 cups basmati rice

6 cups water

3 teaspoons salt

3 tablespoons milk

1 teaspoon saffron threads

2 large yellow onions

4 tablespoons ghee

1 (1½-inch) piece fresh ginger, peeled and coarsely chopped

7 or 8 cloves garlic, coarsely chopped

1 medium tomato, quartered

1 tablespoon plain yogurt, store-bought or homemade (page 26)

2 tablespoons garam masala, store-bought or homemade (page 34)

1 tablespoon ground coriander

1 to 1½ teaspoons ground Indian red chile*

½ teaspoon turmeric

3 (1½-pound) Cornish hens, cut into 6 to 8 pieces each (see page 21)

¼ cup cashews

¼ cup golden raisins

3 or 4 serrano chiles, halved lengthwise

1 tablespoon pandanus essence*

Whenever I have a large dinner party or offer a menu for catering, I find myself preparing chicken biryani. It is a festive dish and I like to add cashews and raisins to it. It is perfect to serve with just a green salad and raita (page 28). I use Cornish hens for this recipe, as they are closer to the size of chickens in India, but you could substitute chicken pieces—buy the smallest bone-in pieces, and if using breast pieces, cut them in half.

Biryanis are traditionally cooked in large shallow braziers, sealed with wheat dough to trap the steam—a method called *dum pukht*, from the time of the Mughal dynasty, five hundred years ago. By sealing the insert with foil, we accomplish the same and save on having to clean up the baked-on dough.

.... SERVES 6 TO 8 ....

In a bowl, wash the rice gently in several changes of cold water until the water runs clear. Drain it and soak it in warm water for 20 to 30 minutes. Boil 6 cups of water in a large saucepan. Add 1 teaspoon of the salt when the water comes to a full boil. Add the rice and stir a few times, cooking it for 4 to 5 minutes, until it is two-thirds cooked. (The longer the rice has soaked, the less time it will take to cook.) Drain the rice in a sieve, run cold water through it for a minute and then spread it on a large platter or cookie sheet to cool. Set aside. Heat the milk over low heat in a small pan until warm to the touch; remove from the heat and add the saffron threads to bloom. Set aside.

Slice 1 onion and coarsely chop the other. In a skillet, heat 3 tablespoons of the ghee over high heat and fry the sliced onion, stirring constantly, until dark brown and crisp, 8 to 10 minutes. Leaving as much of the ghee as possible in the skillet, transfer the browned onions with a slotted spoon to a paper towel–lined plate and set aside.

continued
::::::::::::::::::::::::::::::::

Chicken Layered with Rice, continued

Add the chopped onion to the same skillet and sauté over medium-high heat until it is lightly browned, 6 to 8 minutes. Transfer these browned chopped onions, along with the ghee from the skillet, to the bowl of a food processor. Add the ginger, garlic, and tomato and process into a paste. Add the yogurt along with the garam masala, coriander, red chile, turmeric, and 1 teaspoon of the salt and process to blend for 1 minute. Transfer the marinade to a large mixing bowl and add the Cornish hen pieces. Sprinkle with the remaining 1 teaspoon salt, mix well to coat, and set aside for 30 minutes.

Heat the slow cooker on high for 15 minutes before use. Spread the remaining tablespoon of ghee on the bottom and 1 inch up the sides of the slow cooker insert. Layer the marinated hen pieces evenly, and use a wet paper towel to clean any marinade off the sides of the insert before continuing.

Sprinkle half the fried onion slices over the hens, then half the saffron milk along with some of the strands, half the cashews and raisins, and half the sliced serrano chiles. Cover these ingredients with all of the rice and repeat with the remaining fried onions, saffron, cashews, raisins, and chiles. Sprinkle the pandanus essence evenly all over the top.

Cover the insert of the slow cooker with aluminum foil, and fold the foil over the sides of the slow cooker. Place the lid on the cooker and cook on low for 4 hours.

Remove the insert from the cooker and let the biryani stand for about 5 minutes. Serve hot.

PINK LENTILS AND RICE WITH MINT
masoor aur pudine khichdi

1 cup pink lentils*

1⅓ cups basmati rice

4 teaspoons ghee

3¼ cups hot water, plus
1 tablespoon water

2 bay leaves

½ teaspoon turmeric

1 teaspoon ground
Indian red chile*

1½ teaspoons salt

1 teaspoon brown
mustard seeds

3 or 4 whole dried red árbol
chiles, broken in two

2 large shallots, sliced thin

3 or 4 large cloves garlic,
chopped fine

½ cup fresh mint leaves

During her visits to the United States, my sister Radhika would share her recipes with me. While I was in India during the testing of some of the recipes in this book, I worked with her cook, Gopi, and had fun instructing him with this one.

It is delightful by itself but even more so served with Green Beans with Mustard Seeds and Onions (page 84) and Boneless Chicken Curry (page 55). Unlike steamed basmati rice (page 24), where each grain is separate, *khichdi* is somewhat like a risotto. The preparation of *khichdi* is perfect in the slow cooker; you can cook it in advance and then just let it hold on warm for a while. I like mine where the grains are still a little separate; however, if you prefer yours to have more of a risotto-like consistency, increase the water by ½ cup and cook for an additional 30 minutes and, when finished, do not cover with a paper towel as described below.

SERVES 6 TO 8

Before prepping the ingredients, turn the slow cooker on to the high setting for 15 minutes, until the insert is warmed through.

Pick over the lentils for any foreign objects. Wash them in a bowl in several changes of water until the last wash runs almost clear. In a bowl, wash the rice gently in several changes of cold water until the water runs clear. Drain the rice and soak it for 20 minutes in enough warm water to cover.

Brush 1 teaspoon of ghee on the bottom and an inch up the sides of the cooker insert (alternatively you can spray it with butter-flavored cooking spray). Drain the rice and add it with the lentils to the heated slow cooker along with the water, bay leaves, turmeric, ground red chile, and salt.

Heat the remaining ghee in a skillet on high heat, with a lid handy. Tilt the pan to form a pool, add the mustard seeds, and cover immediately to contain the sputtering. After about a minute, uncover and add the whole red chiles, shallots, and garlic. Brown the shallots and garlic on high heat, stirring frequently, until browned on the edges, 6 to 8 minutes. Add to the insert. Add 1 tablespoon of water to deglaze the skillet then add this to the rice. Cover and cook for 1½ hours on high.

When the timer sounds, add the mint leaves and lightly stir them in. Cover with a paper towel and the lid, and keep the slow cooker on warm for 10 minutes before shutting it off. Transfer the *khichdi* to a holding or serving dish; if kept in the slow cooker, it will lump up. Serve hot.

LAMB LAYERED WITH RICE
gosht ki biryani

2 cups basmati rice

6 cups water

3 teaspoons salt

3 tablespoons milk

1 teaspoon saffron threads

2 large yellow onions

4 tablespoons plus
1 teaspoon ghee

1 (1½-inch) piece fresh ginger,
peeled and coarsely chopped

7 or 8 cloves garlic,
coarsely chopped

1 tomato, quartered

1 tablespoon plain yogurt,
store-bought or homemade
(page 26)

2 tablespoons garam masala,
store-bought or homemade
(page 34)

All over India and in Indian restaurants worldwide, biryanis are served as a specialty. Meat is marinated in a spice mix and then layered with rice, flavored with saffron, and served as a main dish along with Cucumber and Yogurt Raita (page 28). I learned to make it from Chandan, our cook in India, and was delighted when I saw a television show on Indian cooking, highlighting the master of biryanis. His method and mine were the same! Here it is translated to the slow cooker. Sear the marinated lamb in a skillet to remove extra moisture before layering the dish. Though time-consuming in its preparation, biryani makes for a delectable dish when entertaining; the slow cooker insert is also the perfect serving dish.

SERVES 6 TO 8

In a bowl, wash the rice gently in several changes of cold water until the water runs clear. Drain it and soak it in warm water for 20 to 30 minutes. Boil 6 cups of water in a large saucepan. Add 1 teaspoon of the salt when the water comes to a full boil. Add the rice and stir a few times, cooking for 4 or 5 minutes until it is two-thirds cooked (the longer the rice is soaked, the less time it will take to cook). Drain the rice in a sieve, run cold water through for a minute, and then spread it on a large platter or cookie sheet to cool. Set aside. Heat the milk over low heat in a small pan until warm to the touch. Remove from the heat and add the saffron threads; set aside.

Slice 1 onion and coarsely chop the other. In a skillet over high heat, heat 3 tablespoons of the ghee and fry the sliced onion until dark brown, 8 to 10 minutes. Leaving as much of the ghee as possible in the skillet, transfer the onion to a paper towel–lined plate. Add the chopped onion to the skillet and sauté until the onion is lightly browned, 6 to 8 minutes. Transfer the browned onion, along with the ghee from the skillet, into the bowl of a food processor. Set the skillet aside without washing (you'll use it to sear the lamb cubes). Add the ginger, garlic, and tomato and process into a paste. Add the yogurt to the food processor along with the garam masala, coriander, red chile, turmeric, and 1 teaspoon of the salt, and process to blend for a minute. Set aside this marinade.

1 tablespoon ground coriander

1 to 1½ teaspoons ground
Indian red chile*

½ teaspoon turmeric

4 pounds lamb shoulder or leg
of lamb, cut into 2-inch cubes

3 or 4 serrano chiles,
halved lengthwise

1 tablespoon pandanus essence*

Clean the lamb cubes of any extra fat and sinews. Place in a mixing bowl and season with the remaining 1 teaspoon of salt. Add the marinade and mix well to coat all the lamb cubes well; set aside for ½ hour.

Heat the slow cooker on high for 15 minutes before preparing the layers of the biryani. Spread 1 tablespoon of the ghee on the bottom of the slow cooker insert and an inch up the sides.

Heat the previously used skillet on high with the remaining 1 teaspoon of ghee. Using tongs, transfer half of the lamb cubes to the skillet at a time and sear them, turning to get even browning on all sides. Transfer to the prepared insert, and repeat the step with the remaining lamb. Add any leftover marinade to the lamb in the insert and mix well; use a wet paper towel to clean any marinade off the sides of the insert before continuing.

Sprinkle half the fried onion slices over the lamb, then half the bloomed saffron, and half the sliced serrano chiles. Cover the lamb with all of the rice and repeat with the remaining fried onions, saffron, and chiles. Sprinkle the pandanus essence evenly over the top. Cover the insert of the slow cooker with aluminum foil, and fold the foil over the sides of the slow cooker. Place the lid on the cooker and cook on low for 4 hours.

Remove the insert from the cooker and let the biryani stand for about 5 minutes. Serve hot.

GREEN MUNG BEANS AND RICE
hare moong ki khichdi

⅔ cup green mung beans*

1 tablespoon ghee

1⅓ cup basmati rice

1 (½-inch) piece fresh ginger, peeled and minced

5 or 6 cloves

7 or 8 whole black peppercorns

4 cups hot water

1½ teaspoons salt

Khichdi, a dish traditionally composed of lentils and rice, is found all over India. This preparation creates a complex protein and its low cost makes it accessible to one and all. Here I have combined green mung beans and rice, using cloves for aroma and whole black peppercorns for spice. I love eating it for brunch with an over-easy fried egg, or sometimes as a snack with some plain yogurt (page 26) and Chopped Salad of Tomatoes, Cucumbers, and Red Onions (page 27). It is important to soak the beans for an hour before cooking, even though the recipe cooks for an hour and a half.

SERVES 6 TO 8

Soak the beans in warm water for 1 hour. Heat the slow cooker on high for 15 minutes. Brush the ghee on the bottom and an inch up the sides of the cooking insert (alternatively you can spray it with butter-flavored cooking spray).

Pick over the rice to remove any foreign objects. In a bowl, wash the rice gently in several changes of cold water until the water runs clear. Drain the rice and soak it for 20 minutes in enough warm water to cover.

Drain the mung beans and rice and transfer to the heated insert along with the ginger, cloves, peppercorns, hot water, and salt, and cook on high for 1½ hours.

When the timer sounds, turn off the slow cooker, remove the lid, and cover the rice with a paper towel. Place the lid back on the cooker, and let stand for another 15 minutes. Remove the paper towel and fluff with a fork. Serve hot.

about the author

NEELA PANIZ grew up in Bombay, India. After moving to the United States, Paniz opened Chutneys and the hugely successful Bombay Cafe in Los Angeles, and a contemporary Indian restaurant, Neela's, in Napa. She is also the author of *The Bombay Cafe*, which put her on the national map as one of the leading voices of contemporary Indian cuisine. Since selling her restaurants, Paniz has appeared as the winning contestant on the Food Network's *Chopped*, taught cooking classes, provided recipes for many magazine articles, and been a presenter at The Culinary Institute of America.

measurement conversion charts

VOLUME

	IMPERIAL	METRIC
1 tablespoon	$1/2$ fl oz	15 ml
2 tablespoons	1 fl oz	30 ml
$1/4$ cup	2 fl oz	60 ml
$1/3$ cup	3 fl oz	90 ml
$1/2$ cup	4 fl oz	120 ml
$2/3$ cup	5 fl oz ($1/4$ pint)	150 ml
$3/4$ cup	6 fl oz	180 ml
1 cup	8 fl oz ($1/3$ pint)	240 ml
$1 1/4$ cups	10 fl oz ($1/2$ pint)	300 ml
2 cups (1 pint)	16 fl oz ($2/3$ pint)	480 ml
$2 1/2$ cups	20 fl oz (1 pint)	600 ml
1 quart	32 fl oz ($1 2/3$ pints)	1 l

TEMPERATURE

FAHRENHEIT	CELSIUS/GAS MARK
250°F	120°C/gas mark $1/2$
275°F	135°C/gas mark 1
300°F	150°C/gas mark 2
325°F	160°C/gas mark 3
350°F	180 or 175°C/gas mark 4
375°F	190°C/gas mark 5
400°F	200°C/gas mark 6
425°F	220°C/gas mark 7
450°F	230°C/gas mark 8
475°F	245°C/gas mark 9
500°F	260°C

LENGTH

INCH	METRIC
$1/4$ inch	6 mm
$1/2$ inch	1.25 cm
$3/4$ inch	2 cm
1 inch	2.5 cm
6 inches ($1/2$ foot)	15 cm
12 inches (1 foot)	30 cm

WEIGHT

US/IMPERIAL	METRIC
$1/2$ oz	15 g
1 oz	30 g
2 oz	60 g
$1/4$ lb	115 g
$1/3$ lb	150 g
$1/2$ lb	225 g
$3/4$ lb	350 g
1 lb	450 g

index

A
Aloo mattar rasedar, 94
Asafetida, 10

B
Baingan aloo ki sabzi, 85
Bay leaves, 10
Beans
    Black-Eyed Pea Curry, 110
    Chickpeas with Vegetables, 107
        cooking, 97
    Curried Chickpeas, 108
    Green Beans with Mustard Seeds
        and Onion, 84
    Green Mung Beans and Rice, 126
    Green Mung Beans with
        Browned Onions, 103
    Mixed Yellow Dal, 102
    Red Kidney Beans, 111
    Rice with Chickpeas, 118
    types of, 15
    Yellow Mung Beans with
        Fresh Spinach, 100
Beef
    Ground Meat with Potatoes
        and Peas, 77
Bengali dal, 102
Bhuga chawal, 115
Bhunna, 20
Bhunna gosht, 75
Biryanis, 113
    Chicken Layered with Rice, 120–22
    Lamb Layered with Rice, 124–25
Black-eyed peas, 15
    Black-Eyed Pea Curry, 110
Breads, Whole Wheat Flat, 25

C
Cabbage and Peas, Spicy, 90–91
Cardamom pods, 10

Cassia, 10
Cauliflower
    Cauliflower with Ginger and
        Cumin, 80
    Chickpeas with Vegetables, 107
Channa masala, 108
Channa pullao, 118
Chapattis, 25
Chawal, 24
Cheese. See Paneer
Chicken
    Boneless Chicken Curry, 55
    Braised Chicken with
        Dried Fenugreek, 57
    Chicken Kabobs in Green Spices, 64
    Chicken Layered with Rice, 120–22
    Chicken Soup with Rice, Spinach,
        and Tomatoes, 38
    Curried Chicken Frankies, 56
    cutting up whole, 21
    Mulligatawny Soup, 41
    Roast Chicken à la Rama, 60–61
    Sautéed Chicken with Green Mango
        Powder, 40
    tikka masala, 62, 64
    Yogurt and Black Pepper Chicken, 65
Chickpeas, 18
    Chickpeas with Vegetables, 107
    Curried Chickpeas, 108
    flour, 15
    Rice with Chickpeas, 118
Chile, Indian red, 13
Chutneys, 45
    Date and Tamarind Chutney, 48–49
    Mint Chutney, 29
    Mixed Dried Fruit Chutney, 47
    Sweet Tomato Chutney, 50
Cilantro, 10
Cloves, 11
Coconut, 11

Cooking techniques, 20
Coriander, 11
Cornish Hens with Rum and Saffron, 59
Cucumbers
    Chopped Salad of Tomatoes,
        Cucumbers, and Red Onion, 27
    Cucumber and Yogurt Raita, 28
Cumin, 11
Curries, 53
    Basic Curry Mix, 54
    Black-Eyed Pea Curry, 110
    Boneless Chicken Curry, 55
    Braised Chicken with Dried
        Fenugreek, 57
    Cornish Hens with Rum and
        Saffron, 59
    Curried Chicken Frankies, 56
    Curried Chickpeas, 108
    Curried Peas and Indian Cheese, 89
    Kashmiri Potato Curry, 83
    Kerala Fish Curry, 67–68
Curry ka masala, 54
Curry powder, Madras, 13

D
Dahi, 26
Dahi aur kali mirch murghi, 65
Daikon
    Chickpeas with Vegetables, 107
    Yogurt Soup with Daikon, 43
Dal aur murghi ka shorba, 41
Dals, 97
    Brown Lentils with Onions,
        Tomatoes, and Ginger, 99
    Chickpeas with Vegetables, 107
    Green Mung Beans with Browned
        Onions, 103
    Mercin's Lemon Dal, 98
    Mixed Yellow Dal, 102

Dals, *continued*
   Pink Lentils with Tomatoes and
     Kari Leaves, 105
   Whole Black Lentils, 106
   Yellow Mung Beans with
     Fresh Spinach, 100
Date and Tamarind Chutney, 48–49
Dum aloo, 83
Dum pukht, 20

E
Eggplant
   Eggplant with Potatoes, 85
   Eggplant with Yogurt and
     Saffron, 86
   Sweet-and-Sour Eggplant, 88

F
Fennel seeds, 11
Fenugreek, 11
   Braised Chicken with
     Dried Fenugreek, 57
Fish
   Fish with Sautéed Onion Sauce, 69
   Kerala Fish Curry, 67–68
Flat Breads, Whole Wheat, 25
Flour, soft whole wheat pastry, 15
Frankies, Curried Chicken, 56
Fruit Chutney, Mixed Dried, 47

G
Garam masala, 11, 34
Ghee, 15
Ginger, 11, 13
Gobi sabzi, 80
Gosht ki biryani, 124–25

H
Hare moong ki khichdi, 126
Hari moong dal, 103

I
Imli ki chutney, 48–49

J
Jaggery, 13

K
Kachumber, 27
Kadhi aur mooli, 43

Kadu ki sabzi, 95
Kari leaves, 13
Kashmiri baingan, 86
Kashmiri Potato Curry, 83
Keema aloo mattar, 77
Kerala Fish Curry, 67–68
Khatta meetha baingan, 88
Khatti dal, 98
Kheere ka raita, 28
Khichdi, 113
   Green Mung Beans and Rice, 126
   Pink Lentils and Rice with Mint, 123

L
Lamb
   Browned Lamb with Onions,
     Tomatoes, and Spices, 75
   Ground Meat with Potatoes
     and Peas, 77
   Lamb Chops with Browned Onions
     and Tomatoes, 73–74
   Lamb Layered with Rice, 124–25
   Lamb with Spinach, 76
Lentils
   Brown Lentils with Onions,
     Tomatoes, and Ginger, 99
   cooking, 97
   Mercin's Lemon Dal, 98
   Mixed Yellow Dal, 102
   Mulligatawny Soup, 41
   Pink Lentils and Rice with Mint, 123
   Pink Lentils with Tomatoes and
     Kari Leaves, 105
   Tomato Lentil Soup, 42
   types of, 15, 18
   Whole Black Lentils, 106

M
Mace, 13
Machchi bassar, 69
Makhni, 62
Makhni dal, 106
Mango powder, green, 13
Masala chawal, 117
Masala dabba, 9
Masaledar champas, 73–74
Masoor aur pudine khichdi, 123
Masoor tamatar dal, 105
Mattar paneer, 89
Meen moili, 67–68

Meethi tamatar ki chutney, 50
Mercin's Lemon Dal, 98
Methi murghi, 57
Mint Chutney, 29
Mirch masala tikka, 64
Moong aur palak ki dal, 100
Mulligatawny Soup, 41
Murghi frankies, 56
Murghi masala, 55
Murghi shorba, 38
Murgh ki biryani, 120–22
Mustard seeds, 13

N
Nigella, 13
Nutmeg, 13

O
Onions
   Basic Curry Mix, 54
   Basmati Rice with Browned
     Onions, 115
   Browned Lamb with Onions,
     Tomatoes, and Spices, 75
   Brown Lentils with Onions,
     Tomatoes, and Ginger, 99
   Chopped Salad of Tomatoes,
     Cucumbers, and Red Onion, 27
   Fish with Sautéed Onion Sauce, 69
   Green Beans with Mustard
     Seeds and Onion, 84
   Green Mung Beans with Browned
     Onions, 103
   Lamb Chops with Browned Onions
     and Tomatoes, 73–74

P
Pahari dal, 107
Palak paneer, 92
Panch puran, 14
Pandanus essence, 14
Paneer (Indian Fresh Cheese), 31
   Curried Peas and Indian
     Cheese, 89
   Pureed Spinach with Indian
     Cheese, 92
Patta gobi mattar, 90–91

Peas
    Curried Peas and Indian Cheese, 89
    Ground Meat with Potatoes
        and Peas, 77
    Potatoes and Peas in Tomato
        Sauce, 94
    Spiced Rice with Potatoes and
        Peas, 117
    Spicy Cabbage and Peas, 90–91
Pepper, black, 10
Pomegranate seeds, 14
Pork Vindaloo, 70
Potatoes
    Chickpeas with Vegetables, 107
    Eggplant with Potatoes, 85
    Ground Meat with Potatoes and
        Peas, 77
    Kashmiri Potato Curry, 83
    Potatoes and Peas in Tomato
        Sauce, 94
    Spiced Rice with Potatoes and
        Peas, 117
Pudine ki chutney, 29
Pumpkin with Fennel and Tamarind
    Chutney, 95

R
Raita, Cucumber and Yogurt, 28
Rajma, 111
Rasam, 42
Rasam powder, 14
Rasedar lobia, 110
Rice
    basmati, 15, 24
    Basmati Rice with Browned
    Onions, 115
    Chicken Layered with Rice, 120–22
    Chicken Soup with Rice, Spinach,
        and Tomatoes, 38
    cooking, 24, 114
    Green Mung Beans and Rice, 126
    Lamb Layered with Rice, 124–25
    Mixed Vegetable Rice, 119
    Mulligatawny Soup, 41
    Pink Lentils and Rice with Mint, 123
    Rice with Chickpeas, 118
    Spiced Rice with Potatoes and
        Peas, 117
    washing, 114

S
Saag gosht, 76
Saag paneer, 92
Sabath masoor ki dal, 99
Sabzi pullao, 119
Saffron, 14
Salad, Chopped, of Tomatoes,
        Cucumbers, and Red Onion, 27
Salt, black, 10
Sauce, Tomato-Butter, 62
Sel murghi, 59
Sem bhajji, 84
Sindhi chicken, 40
Slow cookers
    "multi-cook," 4
    sizes of, 3
Soups, 37
    Chicken Soup with Rice, Spinach,
        and Tomatoes, 38
    Mulligatawny Soup, 41
    Tomato Lentil Soup, 42
    Yogurt Soup with Daikon, 43
Spices
    buying, 7
    Classic Spice Blend, 34
    list of, 10–11, 13–14
    preparing, 12
Spinach
    Chicken Soup with Rice, Spinach,
        and Tomatoes, 38
    Lamb with Spinach, 76
    Pureed Spinach with Indian
        Cheese, 92
    Yellow Mung Beans with
        Fresh Spinach, 100
Star anise, 14
Sukhe phal ki chutney, 47

T
Tadka, 20
Tamarind, 14
    Date and Tamarind Chutney, 48–49
    Pumpkin with Fennel and Tamarind
        Chutney, 95
Tomatoes
    Basic Curry Mix, 54
    Browned Lamb with Onions,
        Tomatoes, and Spices, 75
    Brown Lentils with Onions,
        Tomatoes, and Ginger, 99

Chicken Soup with Rice, Spinach,
        and Tomatoes, 38
Chopped Salad of Tomatoes,
        Cucumbers, and Red Onion, 27
Lamb Chops with Browned Onions
        and Tomatoes, 73–74
Pink Lentils with Tomatoes and
        Kari Leaves, 105
Potatoes and Peas in
        Tomato Sauce, 94
Sweet Tomato Chutney, 50
Tomato-Butter Sauce, 62
Tomato Lentil Soup, 42
Turkey
    Ground Meat with Potatoes
        and Peas, 77
Turmeric, 14

V
Vegetables
    Chickpeas with Vegetables, 107
    Mixed Vegetable Rice, 119
    See also individual vegetables
Vindaloo, Pork, 70

Y
Yogurt, 26
    Cucumber and Yogurt Raita, 28
    Eggplant with Yogurt and
        Saffron, 86
    Yogurt and Black Pepper Chicken, 65
    Yogurt Soup with Daikon, 43

Published in the United States by
Ten Speed Press, an imprint of the
Crown Publishing Group, a division of
Random House LLC, a Penguin
Random House Company, New York.
www.crownpublishing.com
www.tenspeed.com

Ten Speed Press and the Ten Speed Press
colophon are registered trademarks of
Random House LLC

All photos by Eva Kolenko with the exception of the cover and photos
pages 62, 80, 92 © 2013 by Erin Kunkle

Library of Congress Cataloging-in-Publication Data
is on file with the publisher

Trade Paperback ISBN: 978-1-60774-619-5
eBook ISBN: 978-1-60774-620-1

Printed in China

Jacket design by Katy Brown
Interior Design by Margaux Keres
Food styling by Lillian Kang
Prop styling by Ethel Bennan
Food styling pages 62, 80, 92 by Robin Valarik

10 9 8 7 6 5 4 3 2 1

First Edition